THE
LEFT HIS RELIGION

THE PRIEST WHO LEFT HIS RELIGION

IN PURSUIT OF COSMIC SPIRITUALITY

JOHN SHIELDS

First Published in Canada 2011 by Influence Publishing

© Copyright John T. Shields

To Robin and Nikki,
my most treasured gifts from the Universe

CHAPTERS

ACKNOWLEDGEMENTS

I have discovered that no book is simply the work of the author. It is the collaboration of a community where love and good will come together to guide, enlighten, and improve the final product. In the case of this book, the principal guides have been my wife, Robin June Hood, and my daughter Nikki. They consistently urged me to reach deeper and to reveal more of the inner world that makes the fabric of my story. Robin read and re-read versions from first to last and called Briony Penn for her valuable opinions and advice. Lynette Jackson also provided invaluable suggestions for a more polished manuscript and Donna Morton enthusiastically cheered me on.

I owe a great deal to Sylvia Taylor, my editor, who persuaded me to rethink my original concept for this book and turn it into a memoir. "Tell your story," she advised. The conversations between Sylvia, Julie Salisbury (my publisher) and I at a crucial juncture, put me on a path to a richer narrative. To them I cannot be more grateful. Julie's enthusiasm and faith in this project has been an inspiration from our first meeting.

Acknowledgements

My group of fellow authors who have been meeting with Julie for the past year are a constant inspiration and support. Their encouragement and advice has proved invaluable as I struggled to bring this project to completion.

Paul Bramadat, the Director of the Centre for the Study of Religion and Society at the University of Victoria provided a fellowship to work at the Centre last fall. Having several months to concentrate on writing was a luxury, and to do so in the company of dedicated scholars was a treat for my spirit. Walter Hood read the entire manuscript and was a steady support throughout, I am grateful to have him and Lorna Hood as my champions.

The help and encouragement of friends like Cliff Stainsby, co-workers like Diane Wood, teachers like Gerry Fewster have been a nurturing strength. For the many I have not named, who supported me in this project, I am deeply thankful.

Scholars have guided through their books and workshops. Chief among them are Brian Swimme, Thomas Berry, Peter Russell and Joseph Campbell. These mentors have played a profound role in shaping my quest for spirituality.

ii

FOREWORD

Growing up in Victoria you couldn't help but hear about John Shields. He was frequently in the news then, the head of the biggest union in BC, negotiating equitable salaries for women, non-discriminatory hiring or some other battle for social justice. He would be on the TV at night, his pulpit voice projecting the characteristic blend of toughness and compassion. He never seemed to stumble, lose his temper or falter in his conviction of what was fair. This was never more evident than when he challenged one of his own—the union boss of the woodworkers union—after a trip into the decimated ancient forests, where he felt the union had gone too far in its exploitation of the natural world. It was an act of spirit, one that was characteristic of this priest's journey to stand up against dogma and find spirituality in all of the cosmos.

John was universally admired, even by those who didn't stand to gain by his tenaciousness. For a young woman, his authority and skills of negotiating for equity in a world of inequity, power and influence were aspired to but seemed impossibly unattainable—another galaxy. I'd started on my own little battles to defend small things like wildflowers, oak trees, lizards and streams but I had no inkling that our worlds would one day fuse and that there would be a commonality in our beliefs and ideas.

Twenty years later, John met my best friend, his second wife Robin, and I was welcomed into their orbit. John shared his many stories, the content of which you will read in this book—a fusing of personal memoir charting his philosophical evolution from priest to social rights counselor/activist to cosmologist and nurturer of spirit and earth, with parallel public discourse over the last 60 years in the fields of quantum physics, ecology, astronomy, anthropology and theology.

Many people encouraged John to write this book because he is uniquely positioned to bring the worlds of spirit and science together in an accessible form. He has had access to the theological colleges, laboratories, astronomical observatories, union bargaining tables, parliaments, long houses and counseling clinics where these ideas were formed. He has synthesized these experiences and theories and brought them to us in a way that we can all relate to—a personal memoir with interpretations and applications in a life devoted to service—both publicly and privately. Many of us ask, how do you marry spirit with science? How do you find spiritual meaning in the secular age or hang on to the wonder of science in the increasingly orthodox dogma of religions? How do you take these ideas and then offer them to someone who is dying or has a hungry child or is struggling with grief or difficult issues of governance to help them get through the day?

Cosmology offers such an elegant solution to these questions and this book provides a priest's journey to that answer from his first orthodox training in the Catholic church in his native New York, awakening with the civil rights movement, Martin Luther King and the radical theologians to his encounters with the traditional ecological wisdom of First Nations and the ancient forest on the coast of British Columbia. John demonstrates that we are at a profound point in human history with an ability to know more than we have ever known about the minutiae of scientific discovery and at the same time, embrace a spiritual tradition that bridges the ancient with the modern.

Reading this book is like being at the dinner table with John. Everyone feels included and present in the grand unfolding of evolution. The twin stories of the cosmos and his life, bind us all together with an equalizing force. No matter whom he writes about, from his compromised steelworker father who found it difficult to express his parental love, to his first wife with her mystical struggles, their eyes catch the same sparkle of light released at the conception of the universe. Everyone in John's universe, from the trees that offered him solace during his first seminary retreats to the young woman he came to adopt full heartedly in his second marriage, is made from the same stardust and fuelled from the same energy of the sun. The book is a celebration that all of our emerging consciousnesses came from the same origins and together we are all creating a future.

Many will enjoy the company of someone who has explored the paradoxes of religion and spirituality. Here is a man who was at birth predicted to be the first North American pope but then shed all his early promise and training to question orthodoxy. I come from a long tradition of theologians and missionaries, (one of my ancestors was named Christian Church), so I have some experience in the virtues and disasters of orthodox faiths. My grandfather had been an Anglican missionary in India then returned to be a vicar of a country parish. I only knew my grandfather back in England where he would conduct services of great beauty especially around harvest time when all the local parishioners would bring their produce to be blessed in the old Norman church. My grandmother, who was my deepest influence, had a very grounded simple faith based on kindness to all creatures and humans. When I visited, we walked to visit the woodlands and meadows around her small cottage greeting the bluebells, parishioners and badgers alike. This was my understanding of Christianity, but I couldn't reconcile the damage this same church had and was inflicting on others around the world — especially the damage to the children of first nations back home. When John writes about the crisis of his faith when the Catholic church abandoned the principles of equity and speaking truth to power, I believe many people will recognize that moment of faltering faith, and then the long, difficult journey to find something to replace it. John has put up signposts for replenishing the cup. Anyone from a lapsed orthodox faith will enjoy it. I ended up back where I started as a child — walking like my grandmother in nature.

In this regard, John's story is vitally important for women as for men and for different reasons. Like my grandmother, I shine when I am outside sharing the joy, paradox and humour of my home place with all its warts and wonder. I tried to venture into positions of power in order to protect those intangible qualities — the glint of a lizard's eye, the sweet taste of fresh water, the coolness and light of an ancient forest, a safe wildflower meadow where my boys tumbled in the sun, but the warrior's armour didn't fit. John always represented to me someone who could carry the sword well. But a key section in the book is his insight into perpetuating only those archetypes. It is tempting for those of us who don't see ourselves as white knights or lone rangers, to undervalue our contributions, or worse, to long for one to save us. John's years of self-reflection and personal work explore the archetypes powerful men carry around about themselves and the failure in his own circumstances. For John behaving like a lone ranger or believing the lone ranger will solve our problems is inhibiting our ability to address the huge issues, both environmental and social, facing us. Warrior archetypes that may once have served us well in a different time and place, are not serving us well in the 21st century. John Shields' voice is like the last bark of the silverback primate urging the troop to drop his lone authority and adopt a more collective form of governance and spirituality. It is like the last order but the most important one, and ironically it would take someone of his authority to issue it. The book is a call to men and women alike to assume new roles.

For anyone interested in the curious and frightening turn that society has recently taken—disintegrating democracies, the growing manipulation of the many by the few through fear, ideology and rhetoric—this book also offers a very personal insight into a similar time with the turning back of Pope John XXIII's reforms by his successor. We need powerful stories for our time that remind us of the constant vigilance needed, the advances that had once been made and the shift towards commonality that is required. The cosmological story does that. It is as easily adopted by someone who is deeply committed to science as someone who is bound to religion. It offers the common ground.

Which leads to the final gift of this book and that is the celebration of what an expanding worldview, that celebrates all creation, brings to our lives at both a personal and a global level. Living with an expanded worldview makes you happier, want for less, and, therefore, live easier on this fragile earth of ours. We latch on to personal stories because that is what interests us most and what we can comprehend. But the story also demonstrates that a cosmological worldview could shape a very different collective future. The story of a priest who embraces the scientific revelations of the time and uses them to forge a life of discovery, joy, spirituality and inclusion—of even the smallest creatures—is an important story of our time.

Briony Penn

Best Columnist and Feature Writer in Western Canada, 2001,
Television broadcaster and host of Enviro/Mental, Author of the BC
Bestseller "Year on the Wild Side", published by Horsdal & Schubart

Acknowledgements

1

THE FIRST
AMERICAN POPE

Tell me, what is it you plan to do
With your one wild and precious life?

MARY OLIVER

I

When I was a baby, my grandfather held me in his outstretched arms and proclaimed that I would be the first American Pope.

On May 8, 1965, I was ordained a Roman Catholic priest. The sanctuary of my order's mother church was rich with the smell of incense and the echoes of the choir. Everyone there was embraced by the sense of the Sacred. As I walked from the altar where the Cardinal had just anointed my hands, to the communion rail where my family waited for my first blessing, I was overcome by feelings of awe and gratitude. For me, this was the culmination of my grandfather's prophecy.

Standing before me were my mother and father and my beloved grandmother, the three people who were most influential on my being there. They remembered what my grandfather had foretold about me, and the promise that it held.

Ordination into the Priesthood, May 1965

I had left home at seventeen and spent the ensuing ten years in the Paulist Father's seminary being educated for the priesthood. As the only son of devout Irish Catholic parents, my ordination was the fulfillment of a family dream. For me it was the culmination of sacrifice and hard work, and deep and wrenching change.

Just as I was beginning my studies in the major seminary, Pope John XXIII convened the Second Vatican Council, an ecumenical council that he intended to renew Roman Catholicism. By unforeseeable coincidence, my teachers were priests who had been close to the preparation for the Council and had studied with the theologians who would write the Council documents for the bishops. Vatican II turned out to be the most far-reaching renewal event that the Catholic Church could remember, and it would indelibly change my life.

My priesthood would be defined by my assignment to teach the theology that emerged from the renewal mandate, and a Pope who would destroy my faith by denying the Council's implications.

II

There was no Garden of Eden

The Vatican Council changed every area of my preparation for the priesthood, as it worked on reforms intended to update and renew the way the church acted in the world. I was taught the new rather than the older way of Roman Catholic thinking. My teachers used the text that their teachers were producing for the Council in Rome. I had the opportunity to learn almost first hand the basis for the renewal. Among the most significant changes was the document on Sacred Scripture. The Council Bishops debated and voted on a mandate to change the centuries old approach of the understanding of the Bible. Scholars who understood the philosophy behind the Council documents shared their insights in class.

All the documents enacted by the Council were intended to impact the way the church would express itself in the future. What I learned in seminary radically changed my understanding of Catholic teaching. Over the course of six years, I had to relinquish beliefs that I had learned as a student in religion classes. In graduate theology school, studying the Scriptures, I found profound changes in the way the modern church thought about the Bible. Starting in the mid-twentieth century, Protestant, Catholic, and Jewish biblical experts around the world had been discovering information about Scriptures that was not previously available. The agreement among the experts about the new information required entirely new interpretation of the sacred texts.

As I was exposed to the new insights, I often felt lightheaded, as though I was breathing rarified air. Many of the discoveries made in the seminary shook my faith in the church's infallibility to its foundation. As I studied the *Book of Genesis*, one of the most important books in the Old Testament, I realized how much modern scholars had changed what most Roman Catholics commonly understood.

Scholars had discovered that Moses did not write *Genesis*. Although I had learned in church school that *Genesis* was one of the five books of Moses, rather, it was created five hundred to a thousand years after the time that Moses was thought to have lived and a mere five hundred years before the time of Christ. The scholars also agreed that it was not history.

It is commonly accepted by scriptural experts that there was no Garden of Eden. The authors of *Genesis* were not asserting that there was an actual couple called Adam and Eve. There was no Snake, no Fall, and no Original Sin. The creation accounts were mythic stories designed to teach theology not history. They were not providing a history of the origin of the world.

I was shocked and disturbed when I first learned these findings. Centuries of fighting between the church and science could have been avoided if the contemporary knowledge was available at the time.

What the church had taught in the past was mistaken

When the Vatican Council adopted the findings of the best biblical scholars, the assembly of the world's bishops made a bold break with the past. They asserted that in order to interpret the Bible a reader must understand the literary style, the context, and the intention of the author of the book. Consequently, what the church had taught in the past was mistaken and there was an urgent need to correct the ramifications of these errors.

The evidence that was becoming available was strong and irrefutable. I examined the evidence from history, from internal critical analysis of the texts, and from external historical evidence, such as the conquest of Babylon by the Persians, and was completely won over to the new conclusions. That enabled me to relinquish my earlier held beliefs, which were based on incomplete knowledge.

By embracing the new discoveries about *Genesis,* the Council opened the door to a significant reinterpretation of some of the church's key teachings. If there was no Adam or Eve, and there was no Garden of Eden, there was no Original Sin.

The Council did not deal with the implications of the new understanding of the Bible. This was left to theologians to accomplish after the Council was over. I was aghast when Paul VI, who had succeeded John XXIII, rejected the key teaching of the Bishops at the Council. In his proclamation, the pope admitted that the truth would be too upsetting to church members.

A new explanation of
the Christian religion

With no fall from grace, humanity did not need to be redeemed. The Gospels taught that Jesus' message was a message of love. The church should be re-examining Christ's mission to emphasize the shift from law to love. He could be seen as an example of God's love rather than a human sacrifice who died for our sins. The anticipation of participating in a new explanation of the Christian religion exhilarated me as I set out on my first assignment as a priest.

I discovered that very few priests had been trained in the new theology. Only a handful of bishops put an emphasis on teaching the Vatican II philosophy. The retrenchment to the pre-council positions came so quickly that the new teaching never made it into seminary curricula for priestly training.

As a result, very few clergy were prepared for the sweeping changes the Council had introduced and their resistance to change was high. Most even resisted turning the altar to face the people and praying the Mass in English.

My role as a new priest had been to teach the new Vatican Council theology. The Council was still in session when I began my first assignment. As a teacher, I found that lay people avidly welcomed the message of the Council and were ready to adopt its thinking. The clergy, however, were fearful of the changes the Council required. They rejected the message and the messenger. I was transferred from my post after two years. By then, the new Pope was rejecting the teaching of the Council.

The Pope wanted to silence all the eminent theologians who would bear witness to the truth

The Vatican Curia reacted swiftly to cover up all evidence of the Council's teaching about the Bible. The experts who advised the Bishops were systematically removed from their teaching positions in Catholic universities. It was as though the Pope wanted to silence all the eminent theologians who would bear witness to the truth he was rejecting. After only four years as a priest, although my position as Religious Education Director at the parish at the University of Texas was relatively minor, my superior silenced me because of the effect my teaching was having. He removed me from my role as director and prohibited me from preaching in the parish. My role was over. The church was consciously reverting to an ignorance-based position, and was eradicating the scholarly evidence that would have called them to account.

I was devastated. The impact sent me reeling. Without a parish or a classroom, my role as a priest disappeared. The force of the experience led me to leave the clergy and the church. The crisis started me on my journey from religion to spirituality.

III

Up to that point, religion had been my whole life. I had a personal sense of relationship with God and Jesus since I was a young boy. I had a picture of the Sacred Heart in my bedroom. My mother not only went to church on Sunday but the nine first Fridays as well. My father was not devout, but he would have considered himself religious. Their friends were all Catholic, and they counted priests among their friends from their own pre-married days. I am not sure when I first wanted to be a priest, but I know that by high school I was conscious of a quiet longing. Some people say there are no accidents, but at the time, my entry into Brooklyn Prep felt like happenstance.

I went to the Catholic school in our parish. My family wanted me to receive a solid education in my faith. In reality, the parochial school education was less than ideal. Sixty children sat in desks that were bolted to the floor in rows six across and ten deep. I got very little personal attention. No teacher spotted my dyslexia. Because of the demand for admissions, the school had two entry periods, September and January. I was in the January group.

When I was ready for high school, my mother learned of a school in Brooklyn run by the Jesuits that offered an accelerated program, which enabled students to do the four years of schooling in three-and-a-half. I passed the admission tests. The down side was I would need to commute by bus and subway for an hour-and-a-half, each way. Despite the obstacles, I enrolled in Brooklyn Prep's accelerated program.

The Jesuits, who had a reputation for their excellent teaching, were the teachers there. As teachers and as men, they were exemplary. They were tough if they needed to be and solicitous in their care for their students. For the first time, I had brilliant teachers who took an interest in me and loved what they taught. In first year, I had a history teacher who made American history come alive. I found

11

myself excelling in academic work as well. I played on the football team and was considered for a future football scholarship to college.

There was an unfortunate incident at the start of my second year. During a football game, I broke my nose. I thought it a badge of honour in a tough sport. My mother was alarmed that my face was marred. Any disfiguring of my face horrified her. She was particularly concerned that no damage happens to my hands, which she observed might someday hold the consecrated host. She made me promise to give up football altogether. I felt shame at obeying her. I blamed myself for giving in to my mother's fear. My reaction to the incident affected my feeling of belonging and before the end of the year my grades slumped. I did not see the connection at the time, nor could I talk to my mother about it.

My English teacher that year was Father Daniel Berrigan. He would later become the leading Catholic critic of the war in Viet Nam. He repeatedly protested the draft and served a three-year prison sentence for his courageous actions. He founded Plough Shares, a leading non-violent organization to promote peace and to end the Viet Nam war.

When I met him, he was a young, slightly built priest and surprisingly shy. His angular features and intense manner projected self-respect. I admired him from our first meeting. He invited some of the boys from my class to become involved in social action. He told us about some people who were not getting a fair deal in their neighbourhood. He suggested that we could make a difference in the lives of our neighbours. I enrolled in his program called the Sodality, which was based on the principles of the *see, judge, act* method of approaching and assessing situations.

This involvement with the Sodality seemed like an honour to my family. They were thrilled that I was developing a relationship with the priests and were fascinated by the project I was joining.

Father Berrigan took us to Bedford-Stuyvesant, the housing project that was experiencing what looked like vandalism, and assigned us to observe the situation and come back with solutions. We discovered that the new residents were scavenging wood from banisters and windowsills to use as wood for cook stoves. It was not vandalism, but the absence of life skills that could be easily resolved. I learned that by working with him and the others I could make the world more just. I watched a priest, who was my teacher, influence the world for the better. I wanted to have that influence on the world.

At the end of third year, I decided to try the seminary. I chose the Paulists because of their reputation in New York for preaching and work on the radio. I went from Brooklyn Prep to the Minor Seminary to find out if I could be a priest. My mother was overjoyed that I was taking that step, although she was upset that I would be leaving home to live so far away. I could not tell her that I wanted distance from her tight emotional control. My dad had difficulty expressing what he felt, and he was not sure that a life of celibacy was something he wanted for me. Nonetheless, he supported me to go.

St. Peter's College was in Catonsville, Maryland, the outskirts of Baltimore. I was excited by the prospect of studying to become a priest. Regardless of the legend of my grandfather's prediction that I would be Pope, the ideal work that was close to God continually beckoned to me. As a teen, there was a romanticism about the priesthood. Looking back through the eyes of my later experience, I saw the possibility of living a holy life as the fulfillment of my idea of the church.

My classes were small, only about seven to fifteen men for the next three years. I learned Greek and Latin, and followed a classics course in preparation for entering the major seminary to study philosophy and theology. The simplicity of the seminary routine suited my contemplative nature. We followed the church's liturgical cycle from season to season. The rituals of the liturgy stirred me deeply. I saw them as a portal to a deeper mysticism that transported me into a timeless state. Even singing in the ancient Latin added to the mystique. My favourite season was Easter. The church's reenactment of the death and resurrection mysteries made a profound impression on me. For the first time, I kept vigil on Holy Thursday, kneeling before the altar for hours at a time, a practice I would repeat every year for the next ten years of my studies. I felt an intense closeness to Jesus Christ, the Prince of Peace and thought of myself as following in his footsteps.

Prayer became direct communication. Alone in the plain wood-paneled chapel, my imagination allowed me to develop a personal sense of connection with Christ. The Saviour was my intimate companion, and I spent many hours in conversation with him.

Kneeling in the early morning darkness, I had a strong sense of his presence.

The first few years in the seminary convinced me that I wanted to become a priest, and I was prepared for the demands the life required. The biggest concern I had was the requirement for celibacy. Although I had never had sex, I was not sure I could live without intimacy or physical love and joy. That seemed like an endless sacrifice that might be beyond my capabilities.

Seminarians at the early stages of their education were allowed to go home for the summer, and that was a time to test my inner resolve. My parents had a cottage on Peconic Bay in Southampton, Long Island where I had spent the summers before entering the seminary. I loved the area, especially the open Atlantic and boating on the bay. I had been a leader among a large group of friends my age that had hung out together. After my first year of college, my second year in the seminary, I noticed my friends' curiousity about my new status and their discomfort that I was now different. They showed an exaggerated respect for me as a priest-to-be.

I tried to limit my participation in the beach parties with the drinking and sexual experimentation.

Although I keenly felt the pull toward sexual involvement, I firmly resolved to distance myself from those activities. I had chosen a road that would lead to celibacy, and while I was a normal teenager, I thought it prudent to not tempt myself beyond what I could handle. I was friendly with everyone and still a leader in the group, so they graciously accepted that I was on a different path. Having gone to the seminary to see if I was suited to become a priest, this was a chance to see whether I could live among my friends in the summer and still pursue the ideal of celibacy.

Candidates to become part of a religious community are required to spend a year plus a day in a Novitiate, which is an intense introduction to religious life. My father was concerned that I did not know what embracing celibacy would mean so he financed a trip to Europe the summer before I entered the Paulist Novitiate.

The ancient cities, magnificent cathedrals, the Alps, and the cultural diversity astounded me. I was registered to take a tour through Europe, starting in Brussels and taking me through France, Switzerland, Germany, Austria, and Italy. I devoured as much the culture and sites as possible in two months. On the tour was a vivacious young teacher from Boston. She was only a few years older than I and had a joy of life that was infectious. Traveling with her fuelled my imagination about what a normal romantic relationship might be like. I had a crush on her. But even with the strong pull for sex, I remained celibate and resolved to pursue my goal as far as I could. I returned home just weeks before the day the Novitiate began. I was not able to put my dad's mind to rest that I had experienced sex, but I did my best to convince him that I thought I was ready to take the next step toward the priesthood.

The Novitiate began with a week-long silent retreat led by our Novice Master. He introduced the group to the monastic rule and the tradition it came from. His favourite expression was, "Keep the Rule and the Rule will keep you." For a year, I was steeped in long periods of silence and seclusion in the midst of a vast wooded tract in central New Jersey. There would be no radio, television, or newspaper for the year. One of my jobs was to grade the mile-long dirt road once a week. I would eagerly drive the grader down the hill to the gate at the paved road, shut off the engine, and look out at the world beyond the entrance. I sometimes longed to keep going through the gate back into the familiar world beyond. When I made up my mind that I was not leaving that day, I started the engine and drove the grader back to the house.

Fasting along with extended periods of silence were regular parts of the novice's life. The monastic routine contributed to an atmosphere of order and stillness. My habit of years as an only child was to carry on an active conversation with my mind. I was a keen observer, analyzing what I saw and heard. I noticed that the solitude bothered some of my fellow novices.

Some men in the group could not tolerate the intensity of the internal exposure. Often they just quickly left. Throughout the year, several quietly left without a word to any of us. I found the departures of people I had become close to very difficult. I guarded myself against the loss, holding others at a distance, not knowing who would leave next. As a result, I pulled more into myself. This experience scared me, making intimacy more difficult.

I took long walks in the woods every chance I could; exploring nature in every season. The peace that I experienced in nature sustained me when the stresses of close living grated on my nerves. Because of the rule of silence, I could not resolve conflicts when they came up in the quiet periods. Hurts went on hold until there is a period when talking was permitted. My self-awareness did not deepen perceptibly. My Novice Master was schooled in religious practices, but did not have a developed understanding of psychology.

On September 8, 1959, I made my first promises of poverty, chastity, and obedience and was formally inducted into the Paulist Community. I was given the distinctive robe of a Paulists, which I would wear daily for the next ten years. My mother and father came to Mt. Paul to witness the Investiture ceremony. They were shocked at how thin I was. Afterward, we drove home to Queens Village together. They could tell a difference in me. I found it difficult to make conversation after the year of quiet. They had invited my cousins and some friends to their house to welcome me home. I realized that day that my parents' home was no longer my home.

For the next six years, I would live, study and work at St Paul's College in Washington, D.C. The college was an older gothic-style, three-story building with three newer wings. The college provided housing for students, faculty, and a group of Mexican nuns who cooked and did the laundry. A beautiful two-story chapel occupied the central wing, which also held the massive dining hall and kitchen as well as the common room where the students met, watched TV, and debated current issues. Other wings held an impressive library, residences for students and priests, classrooms, individual small chapels, workshops, and a bindery attached to the library.

The life of the college centered on the chapel. Every day, the students and faculty walked into the chapel before dawn to begin the day in prayer. When the voices of priests and students filled the chapel with Gregorian chant, I felt the sounds deep in my body and I felt connected to God and my community. We often chanted the Mass in the morning and Vespers in the afternoon. I looked forward to gathering in the chapel for these communal prayers.

Daily lunches were eaten in silence during which students took turns reading aloud to the assembled priests and students. I was a terrible oral reader and dreaded the coming of my turn. Because of dyslexia, I compensated by developing a strong memory. The lunch period was usually between 30 to 45 minutes, and I memorized enough of the text as though it were a script in a play. One day, when it was my turn to read, I began to recite my passage, acting as though I was reading it. All was going well until I mispronounced a place name. The priest asked me to stop "reading" and read the name again. Of course, I had no idea where I was in the book and could not re-read the name. I was lost. My cover was blown and it was revealed that I had not been reading at all. It was an awkward and humbling moment for me.

The Paulists were noted for their famous orators. Public speaking, preaching, radio and TV production were integral to the work of the community. We were trained to give an extemporary speech and to project our voices into a large hall. The first time I had to stand in front of the class to deliver a three-minute sermon I was overcome by fear. I stood up but could not utter a word. My kindly professor stopped and asked me what was the worst thing I could imagine. I answered that I would get before the class, forget what I was going to say, and freeze with everyone laughing at me. The priest said that if I could imagine that, the real experience could only be less. I rose up to speak, completely forgot my opening lines, froze, and everyone in the class laughed good-naturedly. It was a good lesson for me: not to be self-conscious but to communicate with at least one other person. I got over my hesitation eventually and became a persuasive speaker.

Part of the speaking experience was to stand on a soapbox in Lafayette Park in downtown Washington. Lafayette was like Hyde Park in London, where all sorts of speakers would address the people in the park on a Sunday afternoon. As a training experience, to stand up on a speaker's platform in the middle of a park and begin speaking in such a way as to draw a crowd is a jump into the deep end.

The priests who were responsible for my training told me they were concerned about the impression I created by my thick New York accent. I sounded like the redneck Archie Bunker from the Television show "All in the Family." They believed that, sounding the way I did, no one would take me for a well-educated person. I was mortified. As a remedy, I was sent to private speech lessons with a highly praised elocution teacher at Catholic University's Drama Department. For two years, I learned to open my jaw and throat, curl my tongue and form my lips to the shape of vowels and consonants. I was coached several times a week to develop an unaccented speech pattern.

The Paulists offered professional counselling to students who needed it. My closest friend and classmate asked to go for psychological counselling. In the early 60s, this was the first time I became aware of anyone getting psychological help. It came as a complete surprise to me. His parents and mine often visited on the same visitors' day. Our parents became friends. He and his parents would often join my parents and me on visiting day. When I learned that he was in counselling, I became very curious about his reason for seeking help. My friend and I sometimes broke the seminary No Smoking rule in a hideaway we found in the basement of the college. He confided his suffering and how the counselor had helped him trace the causes back to his family life. He had made up the story that everything in his childhood was rosy, but as we talked, I realized that was not the case. I realized that we had much in common. I had lived through years of unexpected angry outbursts from my dad. I had to admit to myself that this was also verbal abuse. More seriously, I had lived in dread that my mother was shaping me into her perfect mate, in the image of her father. One of my secrets was that I had left home during high school to escape the claustrophobic feeling of being completely inundated by my mother's attention. As an only child, I was the focus of all the tension in my parent's marriage. I began to get some self-knowledge by sharing my friend's process. However, it would take many more years before I began to do my own psychological work.

In the summer of 1960, John F. Kennedy won the Democratic nomination for president. From the day of the convention in Los Angeles to the day an assassin's bullet felled him in Dallas in 1963, my fellow students and I avidly followed his career. He was the first Catholic to be elected to the White House, and he carried the loyalty of the student body. We cheered aloud in front of the TV set when he debated Richard Nixon during the campaign. We sat up round the clock during the Bay of Pigs and again during the Cuban Missile Crisis.

Kennedy was the first high profile liberal Democrat who could enflame the passion of idealism, and set young hearts reaching for a better world. Because of him, I seriously studied the social teaching of Franklyn Roosevelt's New Deal in the 30s that saved the United States from the destructive effects of the depression. Kennedy was philosophically aligned with the political tradition that embodied using state power to improve the lot of everyday people. My father admired Roosevelt's efforts to end the Great Depression. By studying FDR's policies toward unions and the use of state power to curb the banks, I began to understand the similarity between liberal Democrat policy and the social justice teaching of the church. I wrote my Master's thesis on the parallels between the social justice thinking of Pope John XXIII and the progressive social security initiatives of the Roosevelt administration.

In many Catholic homes, there was a frame with a picture of two Johns: John F. Kennedy and Pope John XXIII. John XXIII was eventually to have a more profound influence on my life.

Growing up, the only Pope I had known was Pius XII. He symbolized what many prized so highly, the unchanging nature of the church. I thought it normal that I would learn my religion from a catechism that was created by the Council of Trent in 1545. My idea of the church was the institution that had received divine truth and had protected it over the centuries. It was infallible when it taught about faith and morals. If I kept faith with the church, my salvation was assured.

Early in October 1958, during my novitiate year, Pope Pius XII died. I was almost 20, and felt that I had lost an austere grandfather, a constant and revered presence in my religious consciousness. For the first time in my lifetime, there would be an election of a Pope. We had no access to TV, radio, or even newspapers during the novitiate year to be able to follow the events. Our Novice Master told us that Angelo Giuseppe Roncalli had been elected and had taken the name John XXIII. I was bemused that the last Pope to choose the name John had served in the 1300s. The choice of name did not signal that he was very modern. I would be proven wrong.

However, in January of 1959, word filtered down to the novices that the new Pope had called an Ecumenical Council, the highest decision making body in the Catholic Church, and the first in over a hundred years. It was a bold move from a Pope considered an interim caretaker. I wondered what impact a Council would have on me as I entered the major seminary later that year. As it turned out, this event would completely change my life. John XXIII called on the church to reform, and to renew itself.

I had no inkling that the church needed reform. My view of the church was the image of an unchanging pillar of stability, uninfluenced by the events of the world or the changing social circumstances. What could possibly need to change?

IV

When the Second Vatican Council convened in 1962, I was just beginning my theology studies. I expected to study from the textbooks that the church had used to train priests since the Council of Trent in the sixteenth century. I watched with fascination as the European and African bishops wrestled control from the Vatican bureaucracy. The Papal Curia, the powerful backroom that ruled the church, had done preparatory work. Observers anticipated that they would dominate the Council to insure that little changed. That was not to be the case.

The amount of change signaled by the work that the new commissions were intending to produce was staggering. My astonishment grew during the following sessions. I had not anticipated how much the world's bishops resented the imperious behaviour of Rome and wanted to free up the church from its effects. Catholics around the world were closely watching the manoeuvres at Vatican II. Unexpectedly, John XXIII died in June 1963. Saddened at the death of a much-loved man I had never met, I wondered what would become of the reforms he had promised at the opening of the Council.

Cardinal Montini, a close associate of Pope Pius XII, was elected Paul VI two weeks after John XXIII passed away. Montini was closely aligned with the conservative operatives in the Pope's bureaucracy. I waited to see if the new Pope would cancel the Council and terminate the reform agenda. Among my colleagues, there was palpable relief when Paul VI announced that the Council would continue. He would take a more active role in the Council, but at the end of the day, pressure brought to bear by the world's bishops foretold that the proposed reforms would be debated.

In that crucial time in the development of the church, I aligned myself with the reform. The theology faculty at St. Paul's decided that we should learn the theology of the Vatican Council. Almost all my teachers had been students of the leading experts who were drafting the Council documents for the bishops. Our professors began introducing us to the draft documents that were being tabled for debate on the floor of the Vatican. Instead of the traditional texts that had been used to train seminarians for hundreds of years, St. Paul's faculty decided to use the Council documents to teach us. Hearing the experiences of my teachers and learning of the thinking behind the approach being taken by the majority of the bishops, I became convinced that the reform agenda was needed and would benefit the church.

I felt privileged to be reviewing the same documents that the bishops were debating and felt that I had a front row seat in making of history. The emerging theology evoked deep change in the thinking of the church and every day was exciting and uplifting. We followed the most recent draft documents and were thrilled that we were reviewing the same documents that the bishops were debating. We could anticipate the impact of every reform being proposed to Catholic belief.

Through the perspective of my teachers, I understood why the Council was replacing the stagnant four-hundred-year-old theology in favour of a vibrant and contemporary Christian faith. The renewal embraced the teaching of the great Protestant theologians, as well as Catholic professors who had attained a strong following in Europe. We understood why the document on priestly training placed an emphasis on the necessity for a contemporary understanding of biblical scholarship. Because so much had changed as a result of scholarly advances, it would have been scandalous if students for the priesthood would be taught outmoded scholarship. I saw the negative effects of contemporary pastors not knowing the breakthroughs that were being made in Scriptural studies. The church's new position stressed that any doctrinal teaching had to be set in the context of sound scriptural scholarship.

As I studied the New Testament, my eyes were opened by how some of the world's best scholars had the deconstructed the Gospels, peeling back historic additions to uncover the oldest layer: the words of Jesus. In my scriptural studies classes, everything I learned in my parochial school about the Bible was being transformed. Each of the Gospels had been compiled over time by several authors, each relying on a source document – likely containing a collection of sayings of Jesus – which was no longer in existence. Each author had a different intent and a different audience to whom he was writing. My early religious education gave me no preparation for the revelations that were part of my training in biblical studies.

My Biblical Studies professor led us gently into the world of modern biblical interpretation. We studied books that had been written on the Bible since the end of World War II. Code-breaking skills used to decipher wartime communication were used to crack Egyptian hieroglyphics and biblical languages. Archeology had uncovered civilizations that shed new light on the history of the ancient Middle East. The Bible ceased being the only window to the history of that ancient era. Textual criticism was improving scholars' ability to trace the development of ideas in the various biblical versions. I was surprised that there were no versions of the Old Testament from the time the books were written. The earliest existing copies date from the second and third centuries, much later than I had once assumed.

I was first introduced to the way that the ancient world imagined the universe, the oldest cosmology, as I studied the Bible, and learned that all the world religions shared the same cosmological assumptions. I began to understand that to interpret a book of the Bible I had to appreciate the way the author thought. I discovered that the Bible was a literary work with different styles and ways of speaking that had been lost over time. My scripture classes were exciting and overflowed with new knowledge. I also discovered that when I went to tell my family about these new insights, they were aghast, not wanting their faith disturbed.

Even in the seminary, I recognized that the biggest challenge for the theologians was the doctrine of Original Sin. St. Augustine lived five hundred years after the time of Christ. He invented the concept of an Original Sin. He was looking to explain his own propensity to sin. The literal interpretation of the book of *Genesis* with its story of Adam and Eve disobeying a Divine order, fit his search. However, in order to use the story, he needed it to be literally true. St. Augustine persuaded his fellow bishops that everyone in the church needed to believe that the First Parents' sin against God infected all humanity with a primal state of sinfulness. The early church also adopted his thesis that the Bible had to be interpreted literally. Now scholars know that the authors never intended to say that Adam and Eve in the Garden of Eden were real.

When I first learned these revelations, I was so shocked that I needed to talk with the priest who was my teacher. What was emerging from the study of the Bible was a picture that contradicted one of the basic tenets of Christianity: Original Sin. It also removed the central reason that the church used to explain Jesus' death: to redeem the world from sin.

I was shaken. For thousands of years the church explained the mystery of salvation based on a misinterpretation of the Bible. The heavy emphasis on sin – so present in Christian preaching and teaching that had shaped my thinking and my belief – was an invention by fourth-century teachers and not authentic to the original meaning of the author of *Genesis*. I also realized that the more authentic meaning would take the church in a very different direction. It would place the emphasis on Jesus' teaching of love, not on sin and evil. I was thoroughly exhilarated by that idea.

Theology students, who knew there was no basis for reading the Garden story literally, could look to science to explore whether we are evolving or whether there was a perfect state in the beginning, from which we fell, as the Bible seemed to assume. Homo Sapiens emerged around 200,000 years ago. From the vast array of contemporary fossil record, the world has been evolving in a progressive direction. The Earth evolved from a more primitive state to a more diverse and developed condition. It did not begin in perfect state that went downhill. There could not have been a literal Garden, and there was certainly no first couple whose descendents generated all other humans.

However, even a century ago, before Darwin, this was not known.

The excitement of uncovering the new information with its earthshaking implications was hard to contain. This was extremely important for the church and for ordinary Christians. I felt like a new dawn was breaking that would bring new light to my work as a future teacher.

I wanted the opportunity to discard the emphasis that sin and guilt played at the centre of the church's view of humanity. I thought that others would welcome this change. I saw the message of love replacing the emphasis on hell and damnation. Here was an ideal opportunity for the church to re-articulate the role of Jesus in history, and to end its fixation on sin and sex.

There were other changes coming out of the Vatican Council about the formation of priests that I wanted to promote. As the elected leader of the students, I met with our Rector and proposed we form a council to adopt some of the recommendations in the Vatican Council document on priestly training. He agreed, and we created a forum we called *Aggiornamento* after the word Pope John XXIII used which meant, "bringing the up to date." We used the draft document on priestly training as a template. The outcome was that Paulist seminarians were mandated to engage in a supervised pastoral activity within the Washington area.

This was a departure from the model that had been in place for centuries. Up until then, those who were studying to be priests were separated from the real world around them. I thought that our seminary had taken a bold new step.

I chose a parish in the heart of the black ghetto. I worked under Father Geno Baroni, a charismatic Washington pastor. One of my first activities was to ensure that all the children in the neighbourhood were given the new polio vaccine. I was visiting a list of houses on a particular block, going door-to-door to give information about getting the children to the clinic. At one house, I could not find one of the families on my list. Asking the kids on the street if they could tell me where to find the family, they led me under the front stoop, into a bunker that ran the length of the house above. The ends of the hall were boarded up, with a door at the front end. There was the woman I was looking for. In this long single room, kitchen, eating, and sleeping areas were open to each other. The woman had seven children living in that space. I was sickened to see Third World conditions as she described staying up at night to keep rats away from the babies.

I could have had no better example of the wretched effects of segregation. In the early 60s, US laws still permitted segregation. Because Blacks were denied housing in the surrounding states, African Americans were forced to find living accommodation within the Washington city limits. Whether one was a well-educated civil servant who came to assist the Kennedy administration, or a poor migrant recently arrived from the south, both were confined to the limited housing in the District of Columbia. Housing prices were exorbitant and rental housing conditions poor.

Fr. Geno encouraged us to bring radical social organizer, Saul Alinski, to the parish to teach us about mobilizing the residents who were yearning for change. One major supermarket had a practice of shipping its day-old produce from the suburban stores into the central city ones so that locals never saw fresh products. We used Alinski's book, *Rules for Radicals,* to run workshops for people wanting to advocate for social change in the inner city.

Because of my exposure to the living conditions in the inner city, I wanted to take action against segregation and racial injustice. It was not enough for me to study the Bible. I realized that social action was also part of my spiritual calling. The day the US Congress began to debate the *Civil Rights Act* I had assembled a large contact list of seminarians, divinity students, and nuns willing to devote several hours a week to staff a silent vigil in front of the Lincoln memorial. We took up prominent positions in front of the seated statue of Abraham Lincoln, who looks up the Washington Mall at the United States Capital. To my amazement, an equally large contingent of brown shirted Neo-Nazis in full uniform set up a counter demonstration facing us. A reporter from *LIFE*, noting the highly-charged atmosphere, said I could make the cover of *LIFE* if I went up to the Neo-Nazis and got into an argument with them. However, since we had disciplined our group to be silent and non-violent, I declined.

That evening, a car pulled up near the demonstration line and a tall black man got out and approached the vigil. He asked who was in charge and I identified myself. He wanted us to know how much our support meant to the civil rights struggle. He introduced himself as Reverend Martin Luther King. I knew this was the place Dr.

King had addressed hundreds of thousands of supporters and delivered his call for a new day of integration. He was one of the leaders I most admired in that era. I had followed and esteemed his commitment to non-violent action to change hearts about anti-black prejudice for years. In the decade of my training to become a priest, I drew on the qualities that King and Beroni modeled.

I was combining my cutting-edge studies with social activism, the two pillars of my view of the ideal way to live the priesthood. In the early 1960s, it seemed that good will and hard work could change the world. Politics and renewal theology combined to produce change in both the religious and secular realms. At that time, I believed that religion was an instrument for the betterment of the world, and I was readying myself to take a leading role in that renewal.

2

THOU ART A PRIEST FOREVER

The source is within you,
And this whole world is springing up from it.
The source is full,
And its waters are ever-flowing.
Do not grieve, drink your fill.
Don't think it will ever run dry, this endless ocean.

RUMI

On Ordination Day, May 8, 1965, four of us from the original class of about twenty-seven knelt before Cardinal Spellman. How was it that I was called, I often wondered. We all went through the same struggles and doubts, the same training and encouragement. On the eve of ordination, I slept little. The magnitude of the step I was about to take loomed large. I realized how completely set apart the priest's life is. There would never be a moment when I was not a priest in the eyes of churched or unchurched. There would always be camaraderie, but little deep companionship or intimacy. Moreover, there would be no children in my future

41

and my family genes would end with me. A specter of a solitary life awaited me.

Ordination class 1965, St Pauls College, Washington, D.C.

Cardinal Spellman would say the words of St. Paul's epistle that day: "Thou art a priest forever according to the order of Melchizedek." It is hard for anyone outside the mythos of Catholicism to experience the way that I was sensing the import of becoming a priest. Culturally, the priest had been the person of influence and often power in Catholic communities. It was not the power or authority that appealed to me. It was the intermediary role of bringing divine blessing to the believing community. Within the religious culture of that time, the priesthood was considered a position of great honour.

My Novice Master often held up the idealized nature of the role before me. He would recite this saying:

> To live in the midst of the world with no desire for its pleasures; to be member of every family, yet belonging to none; to share all sufferings; to penetrate all secrets, to heal all wounds; to go daily from men to God to offer Him their homage and petitions; to return from God to men to bring them His pardon and hope; to have a heart of fire for charity and a heart of bronze for chastity; to bless and to be blest forever. O God, what a life, and it is yours, O Priest of Jesus Christ![1]

What kind of priest would I be? I wanted to embody these characteristics and be an admirable priest, an image of Christ to these times.

Most of Ordination Day is a blur, except for my parents and two segments from the ceremony. The first was the anointing of my hands by the Cardinal and having them wrapped in white linen. The other is my memory of lying face down on the cold marble floor of St. Paul the Apostle church. Fr.

---

[1] Fr. Jean-Baptiste Henri Lacordaire,OP, posted by Diane M. Korzeniewski, OCDS at
http://te-deum.blogspot.com/2007/05/thou-art-priest-forever.html

Isaac Hecker, the founder of the Paulists, is buried in the church, and thoughts of him came to me as I was lying on the cold stone floor. After ten years in preparation, I was filled with the realization I was now a priest.

I so clearly remember my mother and father. My mother, Alice, in her finest dress and wearing a fur stole, could not have been more proud. If she had been going to visit the Queen of England, she could not have been better dressed. Tears dampened her soft and radiant face behind the scholarly glasses she always wore.

Next to her, my grandmother, the other most significant woman in my early life, was also dressed in her finest dress, though of a much earlier generation. She was a large woman in every way. She was the matriarch of the O'Donnell clan that included my mother. Her adult children deferred to her. She dominated their lives as she dominated any room with her dynamic presence. She loved her grandchildren with unconditional love and I always felt special and beloved when I was with her. She held the prophecy of my grandfather in her heart and I believe she always knew I would be a priest.

John Shields with Mother and Grandmother at Ordination as Deacon at
the Shrine of Immaculate Conception - Washington D.C., 1964

My dad, Jack, was a hard-working steam fitter. As
a construction worker, he installed heating and
refrigeration units in the skyscrapers that were
sprouting in Manhattan. He had great difficulty
articulating his love and pride, but it shone from
his face that day. He had often urged me to get an
education. "It is easier to earn a living with your
head than with your hands," he would often
council me. He trained me to be good with my
hands, but not to follow in his footsteps; his

example of hard work and a craftsman's sense of a job well done, was my inspiration.

Dad had been orphaned as a boy, and I knew next to nothing about his parents or their families. He was twelve when his mother died, leaving him and his brother and sister to be raised by cousins. He never spoke much about the people who raised him, and he was very protective of his feelings. He had difficulty talking about his love, but he was affectionate toward me. Although he could be verbally abusive and was a harsh taskmaster, I never doubted that he loved me.

He had been forced to abandon his dream of becoming an engineer during the Great Depression of the 30s when he left school at the urging of his brother and sister to manage the apartment building that was his mother's inheritance to her family. The building failed when the tenants could not pay the rent, and with that went his hopes for a share of the American Dream.

My mother was the most important influence in my life. I loved her as the sunflower loves the sun. Our relationship was intense and complicated. Though I don't remember much of my earliest years, I have a memory of my mother leaving our apartment in the Bronx when I was a toddler. She was a teacher and returned to work when I was about two. It felt like I was being abandoned, and the experience imprinted deeply in my psyche. My reaction was to stop eating, so that slowly over the next year or so I began to fade away. The doctor called it "failure to thrive" though I was likely grieving for the closeness of my mother.

That was when my Grandmother Agnes came to live with us. We had moved into a new house in Queens Village that my father had renovated for us. My grandmother came and nurtured me; loving and feeding me back to vitality. My mother also gave up teaching to stay home with me. I would not have understood then, but she became anxious and fearful, believing she had failed with me. She gave me such constant attention that I too became fearful and insecure. However, by school age, I had become her confidant, spending many hours talking with her, as though I was another adult.

Now, as a new priest, being with my family and the circle of family friends swelled my heart. I knew that I was fulfilling their dream as much as my own. Being a priest in an Irish Catholic family was both an honour and a new level of responsibility. As I drove home with my grandmother and parents, I believed I was different, that somehow the ordination had changed me.

My few days at home were strange. I was surrounded by the adulation of family and even friends. My adult relatives would genuflect before me and ask to be blessed. Friends from boyhood would kneel and ask, "May I have your blessing, Father?" The short visit showed me how much had changed.

I had a few days at home before heading to my first assignment in Vancouver. I would go by way of Saskatoon. The Paulists wanted me to teach theology. I entered Canada by way of Toronto. As I came through Customs and Immigration, I applied for Landed Immigrant status, believing that I would be in Canada for a long time. I would have loved to continue working in an inner city, ministering to the poor. However, my superiors said that they had trained me to teach the new theology, and that was far more needed from me than urban ministry.

I was to help establish a Catholic Information Centre in Vancouver. That would be a perfect opportunity to teach adults what I had been learning. I was also looking forward to living and working in western

Canada since I had taught at the Catholic Centre in Toronto the previous summer. My partner and the lead hand would be Ed Bader, who I had known from Toronto. He had already hired Madeleine Longo, who was well known and regarded among Catholic Centre workers across the country for her leadership in establishing the Centres in Saskatoon and Calgary. At the time, she had been the lay director of the Catholic Centre in Calgary.

Ed recommended that I stop in Saskatoon to attend a national meeting of the Centre directors. It was a wonderful opportunity to mix with the priests and lay men and women who were doing Centre work. I was warmly welcomed at a spaghetti and meatball feast that Madeleine had cooked for the thirty or so people who were attending the conference.

My job would be to develop religious education programs for adults, people who were seeking to become Catholics, and for Catholics who wanted more information about the new teaching from Vatican II. Archbishop Johnson, who had invited the Paulists to Vancouver, wanted us to begin with instruction in Catholicism for inquirers. The Paulists had developed an introduction to the Catholic faith based on the way inquirers were taught in the early days of the church. I was eager to recruit volunteers to be co-instructors with me. This was also an innovation developed by the Paulists in Toronto, where it attracted substantial numbers of lay people. This would introduce me to lay people in Vancouver, many of whom became close friends. I was excited to begin my new work as a priest.

Madeleine and I conceived an introductory series of talks by prominent Catholic participants in Vatican II, which would be given at Simon Fraser University. The Vatican II talks drew consistently large paying audiences. Consequently, I spoke to pastors from parishes in key areas of the city and asked for their invitations to the Centre staff to deliver a ten-week course in their parish. In every location, people fully subscribed the series.

Not long after the series began, I began getting some negative feedback from local clergy. Their comments set up red flags that I foolishly ignored. While the laity loved the content of my course on the renewal of Catholicism, their pastors were aghast at what they were hearing from their parishioners who enthusiastically talked about the new theology. Few priests had even read anything about the new thinking. They had been schooled in the pre-Vatican Council approach. Archbishop

Johnson had not brought the renewal home with him from Rome. Because I was a newly ordained priest, I never thought to offer an introduction for the clergy.

Only a handful of younger priests had been keeping abreast of the new theology. The more staid clergy considered them radical. Many local priests were alarmed by the changes from the Council. They had been trained to the way of thinking that had been addressed by the Council for change. Most were unprepared to investigate the new direction, much less adopt the new theology. They thought the new ideas were dangerous. Many even rejected all the changes, including celebrating Mass in English, facing the people.

By then, I was actively implementing the changes where I could. I abandoned the closed confessional and welcomed people to an office-like setting. The rote "Bless me father, for I have sinned," was replaced by a face-to-face acknowledgment of the consequence of behaviour. If someone was stealing from his employer, he could not get away with "I broke the eighth commandment." When we talked about what he was doing, he understood that he had to stop and begin to make restitution. I would ask the person who came in to confess adultery to examine the consequence of an affair with someone who was already married. Most who experienced the difference commented to me about how much more meaningful their experience was. This feedback confirmed for me why the Council had made that change. I felt like I was an instrument of moral change.

I was a regular panelist on an openline call-in radio show called "God Talk." The show was hosted by United Church minister, Roy Bonisteel, with Walter Donald from the Anglican Church, and me. We drew a large listening audience for a Sunday morning. The lively interchange among us was interesting and sometimes irreverent, but also informative and relevant. The audience loved it.

Monsignor James Carney was named bishop the second year I was in Vancouver. He had been one of the pastors who opposed my work. His knowledge of Vatican II was minimal and he strongly expressed his opinion that I was dangerous. He proclaimed himself a defender of the pre-Council faith. A few months after he became bishop, he called me in to his office to tell me he had requested the Paulists to remove me from his archdiocese. I felt like I had been slapped in the face. I was devastated at the rejection. I believed in what I was doing, and could not fathom that a bishop would reject me for doing it. I felt shamed and embarrassed in the community of lay people I worked with. The rejection of my work was humiliating. I took it personally. Soon after my meeting with Bishop Carney, I contacted Remi DeRoo who was Bishop of Victoria and asked him if I could work for him. He was known to be a champion of Vatican II and a promoter of adult religious education. He suggested that I talk with my order and get their reaction to my plan. We agreed to meet at a theology conference in Montreal later that month. There he told me he decided it would not be a good idea for me to come work for him.

In early September 1967, I reported to the Paulist parish at the University of Texas in Austin. I had accepted the invitation from Father Walter Dalton who had called to ask me to come work with him. He told me he was aware of what I had done in Vancouver and wanted me to do the same work at the university parish. Walter had a reputation in the Paulists as a wise and kind pastor. He wanted to bring Vatican II reforms to St. Austin's parish. Instead of exile from Vancouver, I realized I had been given an opportunity not only to teach about the changes in the church, but also to implement them in a parish setting. Because of the university setting, the parish attracted many young, well-educated families who were curious about the much-publicized reforms to the church.

I had Father Dalton's backing. He announced to the parish that I was the new Director of Religious Education at St. Austin's. He asked me to enliven the liturgy and to integrate the changes mandated by the Council into the life of the parish. The first thing I did was to dedicate one Sunday Mass to young families. I recruited an advisory group of parishioners to help me. Among those people was a talented musician who attracted guitarists and singers to the parish. We brought in guitars, flutes, and drums, to play progressive religious folk music. The group selected lively songs and taught a group of young singers to perform the repertoire. The altar already had been turned to face the people, but I located it lower and closer to them so that it was more easily visible. I spoke the words of the celebration with meaning. The homilies drew on the modern biblical understanding, showing how the Gospels evolved in the context of the early Christian community. Often we would hold a discussion among the people attending, asking those present to relate the scriptural reading to some aspect of their lives. After the service, I initiated a drop-in with refreshments and a chance for people to discuss local issues.

Other Masses in the parish were also tuned to the people who usually attended. The goal was to make the experience of worship as relevant as possible. Word spread, and people came from other areas to participate in our services.

I volunteered as a literacy teacher in the city, and recruited other parishioners to become involved. Blacks and Hispanic migrants who lived in the parish were often hampered in employment by a lack of literacy. My first client, an older woman, expressed radiant joy when she fulfilled a lifelong aspiration to write her name.

Austin City Council had a bylaw that allowed segregated housing. With a group of men from the parish, I took a leading role in a political campaign to overturn the bylaw. The Real Estate industry and some businesses objected, sponsoring a full-page ad in the Austin daily paper naming the organizers as outside troublemakers. I was happy to be on that list.

The parish committee that was responsible for teaching religion to public school children came under my responsibility. One evening, they were talking about the Gospels. After listening for a while, I began to introduce them to some of the things I had learned about the Scriptures. We looked at when they were written, who the audience was, and consequently what the author was teaching. That these were not histories or journalism, and not eyewitness accounts, was a revelation.

The committee members were riveted by thinking about how long after Jesus' death the Gospels were composed. We looked at why they were written and for whom. Why was one so different from the other three? I got them to read the newly discovered Gospel of Thomas and to imagine why it had not been included with the others. I was opening a door to adult religious education. They could not get enough. I was beginning to regain my confidence that the new discoveries were relevant to maturing spirituality.

They began to ask about the program I had created in Vancouver. When I told them that I had partnered with a laywoman in creating and delivering the program, they immediately wanted to bring her to Austin. After getting Walter

Dalton's blessing, they invited Madeleine Longo to come to Austin for an interview. The parishioners were impressed by her and decided to hire her to work in the education program for the parish.

When Madeleine joined the parish staff, we were able to mount a program that addressed both the elementary and high school students and adults. The adult series deconstructed the catechism – the basic question and answer book used in every elementary school to teach Catholicism that been developed four hundred years earlier to combat the Protestant Reformation. It fostered an infantile stance in the learner. Most of the adults who had studied in parochial school had never updated their juvenile understanding of their faith. The course introduced spirituality as an adult experience of inner awareness of the transcendent. To deepen the religious experience of the committee, I began to accept invitations to celebrate Mass in their homes, showing them how the earliest liturgy developed in the homes of the first Christians.

Two events occurred toward the end of my first year in Austin that changed the course of my life, and Pope Paul VI was responsible for both. He had presided over the end of the Vatican Council and was known to have opposed the direction that the bishops had adopted. Three years after the close of the Council, I heard that he intended to issue a new creed and I could not wait to read what he was going to propose. I worried that it was too soon, since the theologians had not had much discussion of how to shift the church from its preoccupation with sin and sex to Christ's message of love. When I obtained a copy of the Pope's new Creed, I could not believe what I read. The *Credo of the People of God* rejected every insight that had emerged at the Council. It went back to the fourth century and reiterated the position of the first ecumenical council at Nicea. To believe the statements in the creed a contemporary Christian would have had to accept the worldview that had been abandoned four hundred years before. It was insulting to everyone who had tried to bring Catholic belief into the twentieth century.

In the prologue, the Pope said he was aware of the pressures that were bubbling to the surface throughout the church, questioning the traditional formulation of the Christian faith, and he wished to reaffirm the archaic fourth century formulation. I could sense the energy being sucked out of the spirit of renewal in the church. He used his full authority to nullify the work of the bishops of the Council.

I was particularly disturbed by the way he contradicted the scholarly evidence about the Bible. I could just imagine the conservative papal bureaucrats in the Curia working on him for the past three years to turn back the clock to the days before Pope John. He made his reason clear: "The greatest care must be taken, while fulfilling the indispensable duty of research, *to do no injury to the teaching of Christian doctrine* (emphasis added). For that would be to give rise, as is unfortunately seen in these days, to disturbance and perplexity in many faithful souls."[2]

At the time, I thought the Pope and his shadowy advisors must have panicked when they saw the extent of what the Council had endorsed. I could see them saying, "But Holy Father, we cannot admit that we were not infallible. We used to teach that we had the Eternal Truth. How can we possibly admit now that we did not know the full Truth? You have to reassure people and persuade them that nothing has changed."

I could see their dilemma. If they admitted that new information had come to light that added to

---

[2] Pope Paul VI, "The Credo of the People of God", Proclaimed June 30, 1968 http://www.ewtn.com/library/papaldoc/p6credo.htm

the way those who lived fifteen hundred years ago saw things, what would that say about the declaration that the church was infallible? Having formally claimed that the church could not make a mistake, how could it admit that they had been wrong? They would have had to humbly admit that what they taught needed to change. Rather than admitting that just as in every other area of human understanding, new learning had added to our knowledge, they tried to say that the fourth century church had all the answers and said everything appropriately. Surely, Christians could accept that fourth century bishops had put their best effort into articulating the beliefs, and could now acknowledge that newer and clearer understanding had emerged. The new information had eclipsed their worldview. I could see why the Vatican advisors persuaded the Pope to pretend that nothing had changed.

It did not seem to matter to him that the old views were not believable in the light of contemporary knowledge. In order to avoid "disturbance and perplexity in many faithful souls," Pope Paul VI consciously turned his back on the modern knowledge about the world and the Bible. By opting to cling to a worldview from the days when the Earth was flat and heaven was a place above the dome over the Earth, he guaranteed that the faith he proclaimed would remain unbelievable. I was irate that in his rejection of present knowledge of the Bible as well as the contemporary understanding of the universe, the Pope engaged willful ignorance. He denied almost all the development of knowledge over the last two thousand years. By doing so, he engaged in what can only be described as a cover-up. In the name of protecting the faithful, he ignored scholarship and truth. He opted to keep the church members in ignorance. By attempting to sweep learning and science under the carpet, he created a crisis for those who had just watched the Vatican Council commit the church to the pursuit of sound biblical scholarship.

Why did this matter to me? Many of my priest associates saw what I saw and elected to ignore it. They told themselves that they could pick and choose which things the Pope taught they would accept. They counselled me to ignore the *Credo*. I had followed the debate at the Council. The vote to embrace the new understanding of the role of the Bible was overwhelmingly in favour of what the Pope was now ignoring.

How could I deny the similarity of this decision to the previous condemnation of Galileo for saying the sun not the Earth was the centre of the solar system? This action smelled of the same error as the rejection of the findings of Charles Darwin on evolution.

I was disheartened by the absurdity of the Pope's position and I waited for the outcry from the world's bishops. There was only silence. I wondered where the collective will of the church had gone. What had happened to my church in the four years from the end of the Council to this assertion of belief statements that I could not believe?

Less than a month later, the Pope issued an Encyclical letter that had a crushing effect on millions of men and women awaiting the update of the church's position on the birth control pill. *Humanae Vitae* (Human Life) would be far more devastating to lay Catholics than the Creed. The Pope condemned the use of the new pill and all birth control methods except abstinence. Overruling the scientific evaluation that judged the pill as acceptable within previous criteria, Pope Paul also rejected the unanimous decision of the lay and clerical members of his own papal commission on birth control. The anguish of Catholic couples around the world was tangible. I had heard

Confession from many men and women who seemed to be at the point of despair over the banning of all forms of birth control.

For a church that was charged with the moral well-being of its members, to deny them access to a safe and legal contraception that met all the criteria of acceptability, made no sense. The local bishop instructed all parishes to read the statement he issued obliging Catholics to follow the guidance of the Pope. The parish priests discussed how to respond to the grim position of Pope and Bishop. All the priests understood that this announcement put married people in an untenable position. We had an obligation to give them some guidance to put the papal edict in context.

I suggested that we remind the people of the definition of freedom of conscience that had been passed by the Vatican Council. Father Dalton asked me to preach the homily at all the Masses on the Sunday following the Pope's announcement. I read the bishop's letter that demanded that all Catholics accept the Pope's decision. I then read the opening lines of the Declaration on Religious Freedom:

A sense of the dignity of the human person has been impressing itself more and more deeply on the consciousness of contemporary man. And the demand is increasingly made that men should act on their own judgment, enjoying and making use of a responsible freedom, not driven by coercion but motivated by a sense of duty [Documents of Vatican Council II, 1966, n., 675].

I ended with the definition of conscience from the Church in the Modern World:

Conscience is the most secret core and sanctuary of man. There he is alone with God, whose voice echoes in the depths. In a wonderful manner, conscience reveals that law which is fulfilled by love of God and neighbour. In fidelity to conscience, Christians are joined with the rest of men in the search for truth, and for the genuine solution to the numerous problems which arise in the life of individuals and from social relationships. [n. 16, pp 213 – 214].[3]

Conscientious people had the right to make their own moral decisions, said the Council, and did not need to simply obey someone else's judgments. I could see people begin to weep with relief during

---

[3] Vatican Council II, W.M. Abbott (S.J.) (Ed.) *The documents of Vatican II. New York: Herder & Herder, 1966*

the sermon. Whatever consequences would fall on me, I knew that I had eased the conscience of the congregation at St. Austin's.

The phone rang in the pastor's office, first thing Monday morning. The bishop, who was normally kindly and open, was ordering Fr. Dalton and I to appear in his office the next day. He was livid. Walter had never seen him so angry. He believed we were defying him. He interpreted what we had done as an act of insubordination and a disregard of his authority. Nothing we could say about what we intended would abate his temper. He ended his tirade by saying that he was tempted to expel the Paulists from the diocese.

It was beyond question that the initiative of Pope John XXIII was dead. The back room papal bureaucrats who wanted to quash the spirit and content of Vatican II had won. A short time later, the Vatican began to silence Council's theologians. Those who were the major influences at the Council were removed from their teaching positions at Catholic universities. I saw the writing on the wall.

The next year it was my turn to be silenced. Walter Dalton was transferred to a new parish and a new pastor was assigned to St. Austin's. He was not long in the job when a contingent of wealthy parishioners pressured him to end the adult religious education program for teaching ideas that were so foreign to them. They wanted me removed from teaching and preaching. It was heartbreaking to see the new pastor knuckling under. He had no idea of the renewal that had taken place in the parish, or the role that the Council teaching had played in that renewal.

The retrenchment destroyed my belief in the church and shattered my sense of spirituality. Instead of representing a church that was coming up to date, I was being confronted by deceit and cover up. The leadership of the church preferred to teach a formula that was out of place in the twentieth century rather than do the work of renewal. I realized that all the training I had, all the deepening to an adult Christianity, all the credibility I put into helping my course participants trust the renewal was wasted.

I could no longer trust the church. The Pope and his closest Cardinals were perpetrating a fraud. The credibility of the church was gone, and with it, my faith in what they had taught me about religion.

Ironically, it was Holy Week in the liturgical calendar when the Paulists at St. Austin's decided that I should be reassigned to hospital and convent chaplaincy. I was not to teach or preach at the parish Masses. At that point, I decided that I could not stay. On Holy Thursday, I packed my bag with the few clothes I owned, and left Austin. As a Paulist, I was given $30 spending money each month. My promise to live a life of personal poverty meant that my community took care of my basic needs, but I had nothing of my own. I had no savings, and no credit card in my own name. I had no way to leave without borrowing money from my parents or friends in the parish.

I had to ask my dad for enough money to buy a car. When he learned what had happened to me he immediately gave me the money. I did not know where to go. I was alone and in pain. Instinctively, I headed to my parent's house on Long Island. I felt defeated. My illusions were in tatters and I was heading back to my childhood home as a refuge. I was thirty-one, and had not lived with my parents for twelve years and not seen them since my ordination. They had retired to a new house they had built in Southampton. They welcomed me without question. I was leaving a failed relationship with the church, but I had nowhere else to go.

I was a priest without a church, but I believed that my church had left me. Everything I had worked for was gone. What I had committed myself to was no longer there. I had no idea what was there for me. I was numb, confused, and ill prepared for whatever would come next.

My mother could feel my deep suffering, yet I could not explain the reason for my distress to her. Her lifetime of piety and devotion predisposed her to trust the church. I did not want to tell her how the church was betraying her. At the same time, she was upset by the degree of turmoil that I was going through. My dad, in his own silent way simply accepted me, without needing to understand why I had left. He was glad I was home.

Day after day, in the chilly spring by the Atlantic Ocean, I walked the empty shore. The gunmetal sky of April reflected my dark interior landscape. I got in touch with how angry I was. I seethed at the betrayal of the truth by the conservative power block. I thought the bishops were cowardly for not denouncing the Pope for abandoning the integrity of the Bible. Why was there not an outcry of denunciation? Most of all I felt personally betrayed and hurt.

Toward the end of the month, I made an appointment to see Father John Fitzgerald the President of the Paulists at their headquarters in Scarsdale, New York. John had come to Austin to mediate a dispute between Ed Pietrucha, the pastor and the group of parishioners who were outraged about his decision to cancel the religious education program. John would have learned a great deal about the value of the work I was doing, but in the end, he did not take sides or make any public recommendation to heal the rift. I imagined that as an "old-school" priest, he would have judged me responsible for the dispute. When I got to his office, he was not there.

His deputy, a man who did not know me, saw me instead. The conversation was very discouraging. He read from my record, which showed that I had been removed from Vancouver at the request of the bishop, and that I had been at the centre of a dispute in Austin. I felt invisible and talking to a stone wall. I needed a kindly shepherd who would read my need for refuge, even if I did not see that myself. In a formal study that seemed designed to convey the power of the Paulist President, I did not find the humanity I was looking for. The coldness of that interview left me feeling like an alien. The image I now had of the church was being reinforced.

I returned to Long Island and contemplated what to do next. My animosity was not just to the Pope. He was the leader of the church that had set out to reform itself, and had wound up revealing a duplicity that scandalized me. I could not see myself continuing to serve that church as a priest.

My career as a priest was over. I needed to leave for my mental health and integrity. I knew the church had a formal procedure for a priest who wants to leave, which involves petitioning the Pope for a dispensation from vows of celibacy and renouncing any future exercise of the priesthood. I had heard that it was quite lengthy, involving appearing before three judges from the Curia. The process requires that a petitioner prove that he had made a mistake in becoming a priest in the first place. Usually the underlying assumption is that someone wants to get married.

I did not believe that I had made a mistake in becoming a priest. In fact, I still thought I was a good and effective priest. When I left the Paulists, I left the clergy. I never asked anyone for permission. I simply left without any formal process.

I was so angry at the church for its duplicity in pretending that it had not discovered that many of its doctrines were not based on fact. In my mind, the combination of the limitations of the archaic worldview together with the significance of the new discoveries, made it impossible to cling to outmoded beliefs. I imagined that because the church had declared itself infallible, not capable of making an error, it was too embarrassing to now admit they were misinformed. I thought it outrageous that the fact it had taught that it was infallible would keep it from embracing new knowledge.

The early church fathers had no way of knowing what seminary students of the Bible know today. The information about the Bible that came from discoveries in the past seventy-five years was not available in the third century. It only became available due to archeological and other modern scientific breakthroughs. If there is new knowledge available, then the most human response is to admit it and begin to incorporate it.

With each step, my decision to leave the clergy was strengthened. It was time to tell my mother and father that I had decided to leave the priesthood. I was not surprised that my parents responded differently to the news. My dad was supportive. He was secretly glad that I was rejoining the world and would be able to enjoy a more normal life. My mother was very upset. My decision was the end of her dream of having a priest son. What did surprise me was that without knowledge about my inner struggle with the church, she assumed that my teaching partner, Madeleine, had lured me away from my vows. The thought had not entered my mind. Nonetheless, my mom was convinced that I was leaving to get married.

She also assumed that I would settle somewhere close to her. If I was not going to be a priest any more, at least I would be close enough for her to see me regularly. That too was not in my plan. My relationship with mother since I was a teen left me feeling smothered. I would need to live at a distance so that I was not pulled under by her emotional domination. I loved both of them, but I was sure that I could not live near my parents. When I told her that I probably would go out west, she simply began to cry. Her reaction broke my heart.

3

THE PAINFUL WALK
TO FREEDOM

*But little by little, …the stars began to burn through the
sheets of clouds, and there was a new voice which you
slowly recognized as your own, that kept you company
as you strode deeper and deeper into the world,
determined to do the only thing you could do,
determined to save the only life you could save.*

MARY OLIVER

I had so many questions. In the days after I decided
to leave, I was beset by fear and uncertainty. How
was I going to support myself and make a living? I
had no reason to ask that question during the
dozen years that I was in the religious community.
Everything I needed was provided by the
generousity of others. Those who contributed to the
collection plate at Sunday Mass or gave to support
the Paulists contributed to my upkeep. I was in a
state of perpetual dependency. The harsh reality
sank in. I would now have to grow up and provide
for myself.

I had no marketable skills. Of what commercial value was a degree in theology? After years of specialized study within the church, I had not held a job in the world. Several more years of school would be required to qualify myself to teach Religious Studies, and I had no way of financing that kind of program. Besides, I was far from sure that I wanted to teach about religion.

Asking the employment question, I had no confidence in my ability to survive in the secular world. Living my formative years in a cloistered environment had left a gaping hole in my development. Out of touch with the opportunities and demands of the secular world, I was unprepared for normal adult responsibility. What would I do? Where would I live?

After the months that I had spent with my parents, I knew I could not live near them. My mother was so connected to me that she did not see me as a separate individual. All through my teens, she was unconsciously forming me into her ideal mate. It never felt sexual, but I did not believe she saw me as I was. What she expected of me was unreal, and not the person I knew myself to be.

Throughout my teens, I could sense that my father resented the undercurrent of my mother's attachment to me. It was an obstacle between us. My instinct told me he resented me for it. When I was still a lad, he would say that I should be more of a man. Perhaps he wanted me to be less timid. What neither he nor I understood was how much fear I had taken on from my mother. They did not have the self-knowledge to know that the tension between them was directly affecting me. Moreover, if their relationship was going through difficulty, my security was threatened. I took on the role of mediator between them, acting the peacemaker. I would wrestle with this early conditioning for many years to come.

I had an unchallenged belief for most of my life that God was looking after me. With the collapse of my ability to trust the church, my sense of connection to God was shattered. That was even more disturbing than the loss of the church. Over a few years I would find it harder and harder to feel any personal connection. As the structures fell away, my belief in God was severely challenged. The trauma of seeing the church betray what I thought was a commitment to truth, was a terrible psychological blow. I had lost my former bearings and the foundation that I had relied on. I could no longer blindly trust that I was living under benign protection.

When I accepted that I could not live in New York, the whole continent opened as an option. I needed to muster the courage to set off into the unknown. I would have to know my mind and go after what I wanted, but that was harder than I expected.

Setting out into the unknown made leaving the priesthood more frightening to me. Not only was I going into a void, but now I no longer had a sense of divine protection, yet another loss that I was keenly feeling. The feeling of disorientation grew stronger, but I did not have the insight to recognize that it was grief. The aridity was another mark of spiritual loss.

My father came to my assistance. He asked me what I needed to take my next step. Where in the past my mother would have been the one to see to my welfare, she was still upset at the idea of me moving away. My father established a bank account for me with several thousand dollars. I never knew where my parents got the money, but they enabled me to begin the next part of my journey. I realized that he was actively assisting me to leave the priesthood and step into the life he hoped for me.

After reviewing the places I had lived, I decided to go back to British Columbia. I loved the interplay of the mountains and the sea, the unspoiled natural environment, ancient trees, and the easy access to some of the most beautiful places in the world. The picture in my mind drew me back.

The laity I had worked with in Vancouver had progressive values that supported collaborative approaches to community. Moreover, British Columbia was rich in the cultural heritage of First Nations. I had lived there and was known in some circles. I thought that I could call on people to help me get settled. However, I realized that they knew me as a priest, and now without that role, their response might be different.

To my folks, BC was the other side of the world. They could taste the loneliness they would experience if I lived so far away. Yet, they accepted it better than I expected. I planned to leave at the end of May. I was surprised that May was the anniversary of my ordination, and it had only been four years ago.

With the decision made about where to live, I began to make plans to travel. I had a desire to talk to Madeleine; I had not talked to her or any of my community since I left. I called to bring her up to date. There was so much to share. Hearing her on the phone, I realized how much we had supported each other during the four years we worked together. I started with my decision to leave the priesthood and to return to British Columbia. She told me that the pastor had dismantled the education program and terminated her job. The core group of lay people had decided to keep together and do what they could to continue the work that I had started. They asked her to stay on in Austin and had found money for her salary. I knew that she had come to Texas to work with me, and that her work there would not last long. I asked her if she would like to come with me to BC. I was delighted when she agreed.

In my naivety, I did not clarify the level of commitment that was implied in my invitation. I had had little experience with women. I did not even specify the nature of what I was asking her or why she was coming with me. I knew that I cared for her very deeply. We had worked collaboratively and closely. Our creative engagement had produced exciting programs and attracted people into a community. Ideas were the currency of our activity.

I had little experience with what was necessary to establish a relationship. Inexperienced with emotional intimacy and sexually ignorant, I did not bring a solid basis for establishing a happy relationship. When I arrived back in Austin, we agreed to tell people who were close to us in the parish that I was leaving the priesthood and that Madeleine had agreed to go away with me. The positive outpouring from the lay people was astounding. They all encouraged us and wished us well. They wondered why it had taken us so long to discover our attraction. I still had no picture of what that meant. We packed up Madeleine's few belongings in a small cube trailer that we towed behind as we headed to the Northwest.

Sex was really awkward. I had some experience of sex, but never established an ongoing relationship, except my working friendship and partnership with Madeleine. Almost from the beginning of our association at the Catholic Centre in Vancouver, we established a relationship based on friendship and a close, working partnership. We both had boundaries that excluded romantic involvement.

After four years of closeness, suppressing the currents of physical attraction, I had distanced myself from any active physical attraction.

The years of consciously excluding thoughts of her as a sexual partner had coloured how we acted towards each other. Physical intimacy during the years of our working relationship would have compromised our ability to do our work. We had no time to work those feeling through before setting off on a long car trip. Talking was always easy, and I could feel passion about the ideas we discussed. Madeleine had thought of me as out-of-bounds romantically. As we grew closer in other ways, she acknowledged that she did not feel any strong physical attraction. I revered her as someone I admired and looked up to, which inhibited my sexual freedom. These complicated psychological issues did not contribute to an easy coming together. I did not know what was missing, and I did not have enough familiarity to know how to handle the experience.

During our travels west, we began to explore sexual intimacy. I enjoyed the euphoria of discovering each other in a new way. I was headed to a new life. I had a delightful companion and the sense that I was stepping into a free space, leaving the trials behind. I decided that we could work out our sexuality over time. In that spirit of hope, we made plans that as soon as I had a permanent job and paycheck, we would get married.

Friends that Madeleine and I had known in Vancouver had moved to Vancouver Island, a 300-mile long island off the coast of southwest British Columbia, straddling the US border. My friend Harry was managing a moving company in Duncan, a community about 40 miles north of Victoria, the capital of BC and the southernmost city on the island. He offered me a temporary job as a mover's assistant, until I found a more permanent job.

The reality of the job market was as foreign as I had anticipated. I found it impossible to write a resume that pointed to the value of my experience. Several interviews offered possibilities. I was offered a job as a textbook salesperson, but decided that I was ill-suited to that work. A Vancouver Island school district was prepared to hire me as a counselor, but I lacked the necessary teacher's certificate to qualify.

A chance meeting with my friend, Walter Donald, who had been a panelist with me on the God Talk radio show, opened the door to the Victoria Family and Children's Service. Walter was a board member of the agency and he set up an interview for me with the Executive Director. An offer of employment was conditional on me becoming a Registered Social Worker – again, a professional qualification that I did not have. However, the universe was smiling on me. The government had only recently passed the *Social Worker Registration Act,* and stipulated that practitioners had a year to register. Inquiries led me to the Registrar, who told me that I would need a Social Work Supervisor's letter attesting that I qualified. I traveled to Vancouver for an appointment with the head of the Catholic Family Services. His reception was a gift. He told me that from his experience of the counselling that I had done for his agency while I worked in Vancouver I was fully qualified to be a Registered Social Worker and gave me a letter to that effect. I only had to wait for the certificate to be issued. When it came, I was given August 15 1969, as my starting date.

On Sunday morning, July 21st, Neil Armstrong opened the door of *Eagle,* the lunar lander, and became the first human to step onto the surface of the moon. I stood on the front lawn of the home of my friends Harry and Mary, looking to the sky. The moment was full of the possibilities that were opening to the human race. To accomplish a feat only dreamed about over the long history of humans on earth was exhilarating. The future looked bright. Madeleine and I had rented a suite in an older home near the edge of Beacon Hill Park in Victoria, and made plans to marry.

I got my first paycheque at the end of August. Madeleine and I took the hour-and-a-half ferry ride through the most beautiful Gulf Island scenery on the way to Vancouver. Labour Day offered us a three-day weekend. It took all I could afford to book a waterfront hotel room for our two-day honeymoon. We promised each other that we would make time for a more extended honeymoon when there was enough money.

Although the shadow of the church hung over our plans to marry, there was enough of the rebel in both Madeleine and I that we agreed to be married in the church if we could arrange it. Because I was still technically a priest, and Madeleine had been divorced, neither of us was legally allowed to marry in the Catholic Church. I got in touch with a priest friend in Vancouver who I knew would dispense with the legalities and discovered that he was willing to bless our marriage vows. The vows we shared were from our hearts, and the love we experienced held the promise of a fulfilling life ahead.

The wedding party was small with only Harry and Mary as witnesses. The priest who performed the wedding treated us to dinner at the top of Grouse Mountain, a ski lodge with magnificent views of Vancouver and Vancouver Island to the west. On the table was a huge bouquet of roses sent by Pat and Will Barber, on behalf of all our friends in Texas.

My first job presented an interesting challenge to me as an ex-priest. I was assigned to the unmarried parent section of the agency. My role was to counsel women who were coping with an unwanted pregnancy. Listening to women pouring out their hearts about the pregnancy was familiar. I had heard confessions and counselled women in this situation as a priest. Now I was in a non-sectarian public agency. I could not impose religious standards on my clients. Most were distraught at the thought of placing the expected infant for adoption. In the late 60s, the prevailing choices were to keep the child or to place the child for adoption.

Abortion was not a legal choice for the women who came to the agency for counselling. From time to time, there were women who wanted help in working through that choice. For the church, abortion was murder, and was considered immoral. However, for me, any judgments I had about the morality of terminating a pregnancy were eclipsed by the deeply human struggle that women were going through in coming to a decision about that course of action. It was not a black and white issue for them. No one took it lightly, and almost all weighed the life of the fetus in the balance of their decision-making.

Inevitably, after a gut-wrenching counselling session with an anguished client, I came away making a comparison to being in the confessional. I never attempted to confer absolution in the formal sense, but I always was conscious of the parallel, and did what I could ease the burden on the shoulders of the mother-to-be.

The agency had an adoption department that screened prospective adopting parents, and arranged for the placement after birth. Within the limits of confidentiality, I shared with Madeleine how moved I was by the suffering of one of my clients, and she confided to me something she had never previously shared. She had had a child that was placed for adoption. For a young woman of Italian Catholic culture, with no understanding or support from her family, the experience was akin to exile. It left her permanently scarred and ashamed. The event affected her psyche and shed light on our private struggle about sex.

I tried to become a member of local Catholic parishes. My plan was to experience the liturgy in each of the Victoria parishes. I assumed that Bishop Remi De Roo, who had had been a member of the majority reform group at the Vatican Council, would have imprinted the spirit of the Council on the parishes in his diocese. He had spoken and written eloquently about the reforms Vatican II had introduced. However, there was little evidence of renewal in the parishes I attended, including the cathedral. I found myself frustrated to the point of anger by my experience. The way the priests celebrated the Eucharist and the quality of their preaching showed no awareness that there had been a major reform of the church, nor did it reflect the theology that the Council had taught.

I would sit in the pew and seethe at what I was hearing from the pulpit. Negative attitudes toward people and archaic understanding of theology left me feeling that it would be better not to be there at all. Madeleine gave up earlier than I in our attempt to savour the quality of parish life. After several months of this experience, we decided it was simply wrong to go to Mass to get angry and Madeleine and I stopped going.

In the early months of settling into life in Victoria, I found myself growing progressively sadder. I now appreciate that I was grieving all the losses I had recently experienced. Madeleine was also experiencing the loss of identity, community, and prominence within the church. We were each feeling more withdrawn and found it hard to remember the dynamic contribution we once made to people's lives.

For me, I had lost the Paulist Community, the priesthood, and the identity I had been forging since I entered the seminary fourteen years before. What had made all the other losses more acute was the loss of faith and membership in the church. The last loss had come little-by-little. I could not any longer believe anything the church stood for. I can still remember how difficult it had been to give up all final vestiges of religion and experience the church crumbling away. What had once been the centre of my life was simply turning to sand.

A low-level depression took up residence in my psyche. I found it hard to savour the ordinary pleasures of life. I imagined I was in an empty vat with no light coming from anywhere. I simply had to ride over the top of the emptiness and get on with living. Nonetheless, it did not leave me.

In the void created by the disappearance of my faith, I began to wonder if all the religions that spoke about spirit and spirituality were in touch with some reality that could be discovered outside the realm of dogma. Is there a basis for a conviction that the world was more than material? Scientists said that the only reality is what can be measured or weighed. Was that so? I did not believe it, but I had no evidence that there was Spirit in the universe. I began to read and explore possibilities.

The distress I felt was settling into my body. I resolved to exercise to overcome the stiffness. I recruited a handball partner. On one particular evening after work, I felt a twist in my back and the beginning of intense pain. I saw my family doctor and was instructed to stop the handball and adopt a lighter exercise regime. After a few weeks of no relief, I was getting out of bed one morning and twisted to avoid stepping on my dog who was sleeping on the floor beside me. In that movement,

I did something to my back that sent me to the floor in excruciating pain. I could not move. I went to the hospital in an ambulance, where they took x-rays and did a spinal cord tap to determine the extent of the damage. I had ruptured a disc in the lumbar region.

The specialist who took my case was a visiting surgeon from Egypt. Dr. Fouad Hamdi was doing leading-edge surgery with artificial vertebras. He had developed a procedure that repaired the disc but did not require the back to be fused or pinned. When he described the procedure to me, I was impressed by his confidence and more than willing to recover the full use of my back that he promised. When I asked him what would happen if he made a mistake, he looked at me for some time and said, "My good man, I don't make mistakes."

When I was coming out of the anesthetic in the recovery room, I had a vision of a V shape pointed down at the point of the pain. In the V were the faces of clients, union colleagues, and many people in my life making demands. It was so clear that the rupture of the disc was related to the pressure I put myself under. The vision gave me a new appreciation for the connection between my inner and outer world.

I was only out of the hospital a short while when my mother called to tell me my father was dying. She did not think that he had much more time. She knew of my surgery and I told her that Madeleine and I would be there right away as long as the doctor said I could fly. A few days later, we were in dad's room in Southampton Hospital. He was under a plastic tent with oxygen tubes helping him breathe. When he saw me, he signaled that he wanted me to open the plastic flap and I did. Each breath was a struggle, and speaking very difficult for him. He beckoned me to come closer to him, and when I did he reached up, put his arms around my neck, and hugged me for the longest time. He brought his lips to my ear, and whispered, "I love you." He had never said those words to me since I became a teen. Tears streamed down my face as I acknowledged him and told him that I loved him with all my heart.

Madeleine and I were alone with my dad. She told me later that she could not believe her eyes. I had been bending forward over my dad who was lying on his bed. She said that she was sure the posture would be very painful for me, especially in the early stage of recovery. I told her that I was completely unaware of myself, and could only experience my closeness to my father in his last hours. I stayed with him for several hours, mostly in silent communion. When the staff told us it was time to go, I told my dad that I would see him tomorrow. That night he died in the small hours of the morning.

We stayed on with my mother and helped her through the funeral Mass in Southampton. My mother was devastated. She had been caring for dad for several years and he had been the sole focus of days. Now she was arranging to bury the man who had been her life partner for almost forty years. She wanted to have a funeral service at the parish church in Southampton where they had retired and Queens Village where they spent most of their lives. I had said my first Mass as a priest in that church. Madeleine and I accompanied her to both. At each service, old friends consoled her, and depending on how close they were, she broke down and let her tears flow.

We accompanied my father's body to the cemetery where he was buried next to my grandfather and grandmother, and three of mom's brothers. I was shocked to see that she had chiseled both my father and her name on the granite stone. There was a place reserved for her beside him. It was very hard to leave her alone in that vulnerable state. I invited her to return and stay with us in Victoria, but she declined outright. Despite all the times we had visited while my dad was alive, whether at out home in Victoria or in Southampton, my mother still harboured a resentment of Madeleine for, as she thought, luring me out of the priesthood. Their relationship remained formal and testy. However, she was my mom, and I hated the idea of leaving her alone, but I knew that she would never want to live with us. My time was limited, and we eventually had to leave.

My father's death deeply affected me. Even though he had chronic emphysema, I had not been prepared for him to die at what seemed an early age. I had been deeply touched by his giving voice to his love for me, and I suspect that the depth of feeling he expressed made his passing even more poignant. I needed help to go through grieving again. I held a lot inside, and tried to cope with a brave front. I could not do it. I was not coping very well at work or at home. I had become the supervisor of a social work team responsible for the protection of abused and neglected children. My recollection of the times of angry verbal abuse I received from my father complicated the mix of feelings that I had to sort through.

My friend Graham Miles, a psychiatrist who had worked with me to help many disturbed children, was a kind and helpful counsellor for me. I was acutely aware that my principal anchor in the world was gone. I felt like an orphan. As long as my father was alive I had a foundation to stand on. With him gone I was not sure I had a base. At that time, I was sharply missing the comfort that belief in heaven and eternal life had given people I had ministered to as a priest. I did not have any way of believing in the teaching of the church that had been so false in its recent behaviour. It was the first time that I would seek psychiatric help, and I did not realize how much it could help.

I came to accept that I was now the adult in the way I had reserved for my father. I needed to step fully into the responsibility of being a man who could stand on his own feet. I grew up in my acceptance of myself. But I longed all the more for some spiritual reassurance. The church could not provide it, and I had not discovered a basis for spirituality apart from the church.

A few years after my father died, my mother surprised me by saying she wanted to come for a visit. Mom and her friend Ellen, who had taught school together when they were both young teachers, wanted to come for a visit for a few weeks. I was not sure how we would manage that visit since Madeleine and I were both working, and nothing had happened to thaw the tension between her and my mom.

Nonetheless, I was happy that she had relented enough to visit on her own. She said that she and Ellen would love to visit the Worlds Fair in Spokane, Washington. I took time off work to drive them. The drive through the Cascade Mountains to eastern Washington was beautiful and I thought they would enjoy the trip.

While I was driving, I had the most unnerving experience. The two women were sitting in the back seat of my car deeply engaged in conversation with each other. Simply listening to the conversation between them I found myself growing more and more angry until I was in a seething rage. As far as I could tell, there was nothing in the content of their conversation that would provoke such angry feelings. I did not speak or reveal how angry I became and contained the feeling. As I examined the events to find what had triggered my rage, I was unable to identify anything in my experience. My feelings were so intense I thought I was going mad.

During the rest of the visit, the experience did not recur, but my concern about my sanity remained. I confided in Madeleine as soon as I got back to Victoria and after my mother and Ellen left for New York, I resolved to address the experience. I had heard good reports from colleagues about the work being done by Doctors Ben Wong and Jock McKeen. Ben was a well-known child psychiatrist in Vancouver, and Jock was a medical doctor with a specialty in Chinese medicine. They were giving a public lecture about the groundbreaking work they were doing in group therapy. I resolved to attend their talk. They talked about the nature of their group work, concluding with information about a workshop they would conduct that weekend. I enrolled. They had a room at the university and about twenty people, mostly young women, were there. What was unique for me about their work was the body-centred focus of their work. They were able to identify blocked areas in the flow of energy that they called Chi. They released the blocks through having the participant do very deep breathing and used physical pressure or acupuncture to release the block. Participants who volunteered to be subjects experienced intense release of physical and emotional energy. The intensity of the catharsis terrified me and I held back from volunteering during the time available. I did, however, stiffen my resolve and signed up for a week-long workshop at Cold Mountain, a therapeutic retreat centre on Cortes Island, several hours north of Victoria, between Vancouver Island and the mainland.

When I got to Cold Mountain there were close to forty men and women registered for the "Come Alive" workshop. Ben and Jock arranged us in a large circle. They already knew a good number of participants who had been patients of theirs in Vancouver. The bodywork began right away with the first volunteer lying on a mat in the centre of the circle. The two doctors and an assistant worked above his body, scanning for blocks. They began the release process that was accompanied by an horrific release of anguish and then intense sobbing. When the emotion was spent, the man talked about the experience to Ben, who tenderly embraced him. The two therapists then asked the circle to gather round the man, holding him in a collective embrace. I was enthralled. I could not shift my gaze away for a minute, and I thought I was observing a healing that was akin to an exorcism, except that it was entirely without any religious overtones. There were at least two participants worked on each morning, afternoon, and evening session. Sometimes the emotion of the volunteer in the centre touched a chord in me, so that my reciprocal emotion was released automatically.

I had held back, as I often did in my life, afraid to step forward. As I sat observing someone else work, the other man's work deeply touched me. I was crying quietly. One of the people assisting the leaders asked me if I was ready to do my work. I agreed. I came forward and lay down on a mattress in the centre of the circle. The leaders got me to breathe deeply. They encouraged me to imagine filling my body completely with my breath. My body began to vibrate and warmth spread out into my limbs, my hands, and feet. I watched Ben and Jock pass their hands up and down a few inches above my body, sensing any areas where there was a temperature or energy change. They conferred with each other as they worked. They focused on my thighs. They began to apply pressure on my legs, going deep into the large muscles. I screamed with the pain from the pressure.

Suddenly, I was flooded with excruciating feelings of abandonment and forlornness. The intensity was stronger than any emotion I had previously experienced. In the midst of the rush of emotion, I had a visual memory. I pictured myself walking behind the legs of a woman dressed in skirt, stockings, and heels. She went out a door that closed in my face.

As I fully felt the feelings, I had a huge sense of release and elation. I felt like I was bouncing off the ceiling. As the work concluded, the group gathered around me, lifted me into a cradle made by their joined hands and arms, and rocked me gently. I felt comforted and cared for. In the background music played that soothed my emotions. It was an ecstatic feeling.

There were other times that week that I also got in touch with the intensity of my stored-up anger. It was related to the sense of abandonment, and its power scared me with its intensity. I was assisted to release it safely, with no one being alarmed by what I was releasing.

After the workshop, I phoned my mother and asked if my memory rang a bell with her. She told me that she keenly recalled a time when I was about two that she went back to teaching. She had hired a caregiver to look after me. She recalled that every day she felt distressed at having to leave me, and I was upset at her leaving.

I figured out that I experienced that event as being abandoned. Because that feeling was so huge, as an infant I had no way of dealing with the belief I formed about abandonment. The feelings were too intense for a two-year-old and instead of being experienced, they lodged in my musculature. When I got in touch with it and felt the emotion through the circle work, it came back as a current experience. That experience had major ramifications. Anytime I sensed any hint of being left out, or not included, the present time experience echoed into the past and magnified so that the event had greater than appropriate significance. The recollection of abandonment is very significant in my life, and only recently have I been able to release that primal fear.

I began to see the importance of my inner experiences. I discussed the insights and the process with Madeleine, and it seemed to shed light on things she observed but had no context for. New awareness of how much my inner experience coloured how I saw the outer world, and visa versa, began my need to do more inner work. My Cold Mountain work began a new phase for me. I did several more workshops dealing with the anger I had never admitted or expressed. I had repressed anger toward both my parents, but it was more complicated with my mother. I was never allowed to express angry feelings as a child, and when I was angry with my mother, I could only keep it inside. Expressing taboo feelings with others who had similar experiences as witnesses made the release easier. I was not the only one who went through those feelings. I also spent a week dealing with sex and identity. The complications of years of repressing sexual feelings played havoc with me all those years later. The discovery of my awkwardness with women really helped gain some freedom in my relationship with Madeleine, and subsequently, with lovers.

I heard the well-known musician Paul Horn give a talk about Transcendental Meditation. He extolled the value of stilling the mind and finding the core of peace within. I was entranced by the idea. The Beatles had discovered Maharishi Mahesh Yogi, the founder of TM. I wanted to learn to meditate. There was a TM centre in Victoria and I joined a class for beginners. The instructor gave me basic lessons on how to still the incessant thoughts that come into the mind, and how to go into the silence of a quiet mind. I was given a mantra, a Sanskrit word that did not have a translation. By repeating the word, the mind has a focus, and that helps in the quieting process. I adopted the practice of morning and evening, allowing my mind to quiet down and to seek out the source of all potential. It made an enormous difference in me.

In the years to come, my meditation practice did wonders to keep me calm and centred, reducing stress and enabling me to concentrate more clearly. Realizing that the voice in my head had nothing to do with reality, I began to realize the extent to which I was co-creating my reality. I came to understand how much was going on in my mind that was just the product of my thoughts, and at the same time, my thoughts have the power to create what I interpret as reality. This awareness gave me much more of a sense of responsibility for my thoughts.

The outer shell of my religious formation was beginning to crack away. Although I had abandoned religion, it was still governing my thinking. The constraints of my belief system were all adopted, so that they became mine. I realized that they had come in from outside and I had not chosen them. I was not my beliefs. I was not my religion or my morality. I had choice. I was responsible for my behaviour. The code of religion provided neither right nor wrong. I did not have to uphold it and I did not have to reject it. This was huge inner freedom. This was not yet a new spirituality, but it began the process of looking in the right direction.

These insights had the effect of making me more aware of my inner impulses. I was entertaining the view that there is no objective right or wrong. The idea of a Divine Lawgiver is bound up with the Judeo/Christian mind. It was also one side of the debate in the early church between those who adopted the approach that morality was found in the following of rules, and the approach attributed to Jesus in the Gospels that the whole of the law was contained in the idea of love: love God and your fellow humans. However, I was not approaching this in an academic sense. I wanted to free myself from all vestiges of superstition that I had simply accepted as a package. What was good for me? How should I act toward others, and why? These were my real questions.

This was a significant step beyond mere rejection of belief. In many ways the culture of North America was a secular form of Judeo/Christian culture. The inner expectations are tied to the religious forms of the past, and even though more and more people are rejecting the outer form, they still wrestle with the inner mandates.

In the 70s, my work involved a lot of family counselling. My heart was often touched by the pain I contacted in the people who came to see me. I was often attracted to women and believed that I could help them. There was at times a strong current of sexual drive. One of my clients was a single parent who was unable to manage one of her two children and the ministry had taken the child into care. The mother developed a strong attraction to me, and I found her very desirable. From the outset, I knew that it would be unethical for me to become intimate with her because of the power relationship that existed with me having control over the life of her child. The rational awareness did nothing to minimize the strength of the attraction. I usually limited my contact to the office with the door open and always had someone else in the vicinity as a safeguard.

On one occasion, the after hours duty worker contacted me to deal with one of my client's children who had been picked up by the police. The duty worker asked me to bring the child home to her mother. The mother was upset by the child's behaviour, and rather than making an office appointment, I accepted a cup of coffee and an invitation to talk to her at once. The sexual energy between us became evident before very long. I had all I could do not to succumb to my overwhelming urges. I wanted her and it was clear she wanted me. I almost wound up bolting from the house. I felt as guilty as if I had had sex with her. An observer might have laughed at the scene, but to me it was unnerving and embarrassing. I had to transfer the child to another worker to avoid the necessity of continuing contact with the mother. She began to call me at home, to send me presents, to invite me to come to her church with her. I had not talked with Madeleine about the experience, and this further complicated the dynamic. I felt trapped. In order to establish a safe boundary, I had to be firm to the point of rudeness.

There was no questioning the power of the attraction and it could easily have led me into an obsession. I was torn between desire and the need for self-preservation. I knew the rule, but it was easy to make rationalizations to excuse myself. My own urges and attraction made the situation explosive, but I realized that if I crossed the invisible line my career could be terminated. I was married, but that was not enough to make any difference. I did not feel noble and certainly not in charge of the situation. I wound up rejecting her in a harsh way, which was the last thing I really wanted.

As the decade came to a close, and I more consciously weighed whether to adhere to the moral code that had been part of my Christian upbringing, I entertained the possibility of doing otherwise. In the incident I just described, the power of the sexual allure was intensified by the lack of conscious freedom of choice. I believed that I did not have a choice, so that the erotic became hyper-charged. What the experience also awakened in me was the absence of a satisfying sex life. I could rationalize that our relationship was not based on sex but on friendship, and that was true. What I was not acknowledging was that the sex was missing. While so much of the relationship was satisfying as soul mates, the sexual urges were growing stronger. My self-image as person in control of my passions constrained my behaviour. However, feelings that are not acknowledged and dealt with have a way of becoming stronger and blowing up in ways that are unexpected. An affair with a colleague was about to emerge.

I had become a supervisor of a social service office with twenty staff reporting to me. We were responsible for child welfare service and income assistance. The office did community development work in the area and was running a successful program of parent education and preventative intervention. I reached out in love and tenderness to one of the staff, a single mother with one child at home. Again, I found myself limiting my freedom, contending with the rule that it was inappropriate to become intimate with a subordinate. To betray my wife was wrong in my value system, and it was wrong to enter an affair that could injure a number of people. I understood that but it did not constrain my behaviour.

The emptiness I was feeling, the loss of my spiritual compass, and my underdeveloped sexual maturity all conspired to blind me for quite a while. When I told Madeleine that I was going to leave her, I was pierced by the hurt in her eyes. I experienced in one brief moment the pain I was causing. This was stronger and more compelling than any rationalization I did in my head. I realized that I could not enter another relationship unless I had come to terms with the relationship I had with Madeleine. I could not go through with a separation. I loved her and was committed to her. At the same time, the pull toward this lovely and sensitive young woman was overpowering. I wanted nothing more than to be with her. Everything about her called to me.

When I reflect on the power of my mind to create my world, nothing now could be clearer. I chose to be attracted to a person I knew I was not free to pursue. I was married, she was my employee and we were constrained by ethical as well as employment rules. I was being recklessly rebellious. I was ignoring my conscience. In the end I did not go through with the affair. There was pain and learning in this. Both Madeleine and the other woman suffered from my behaviour. I was acting in self-induced blindness that could have been much more destructive than it turned out. I knew that I needed to find a way to be sexual without being hurtful of others. It would need a major adjustment in my relationship with Madeleine, and I would have to be more careful about who I became involved with.

Madeleine and I did find a compromise in time, but not for quite a while. I realized that I was still in a relationship with Madeleine and that I would honour that. I despised myself for not being straight and open. I would find a way to correct that as well. I would never again hurt her the way that I had. I did not really want a separation, but rather a way to honour my wife without sacrificing myself. We did find a way to do more than compromise. It would come in the context of my aspiration to become a leader at a higher level than a social work supervisor. I had the opportunity to run for president of a large provincial union with its headquarters in another city than where we lived. I had stumbled badly in the darkness of my own inner landscape. I was on my way to freedom, but I had not reached there yet.

4

AN UNUSUAL
SPIRITUAL PATH

*A hero ventures forth from the world of common day
into a region of supernatural wonder: fabulous forces are
there encountered and a decisive victory is won: the hero
comes back from this mysterious adventure with the
power to bestow boons on his fellow man.*[4]

JOSEPH CAMPBELL

Twenty-five years of my life, I walked a path that
few would consider part of the spiritual journey. I
was a union activist and then the elected head of the
BC Government and Service Employees Union

---

[4] Joseph Campbell. *The Hero with a Thousand Faces*. Novato,
California: New World Library, 2008, p. 23.

In *The Hero with a Thousand Faces*, Joseph Campbell described
a pattern that each of us follows in our personal journey.
Campbell's template is useful as I describe my struggle to
capture of the grail, recover a sense of personal spirituality,
and to bring benefit to the people I served. The mythic hero's
journey is my metaphor as I select some of the highlights.

(BCGEU). For me, this was the context of my greatest learning, as well as my toughest challenges.

Election as BCGEU President June 1985

When I started out in Social Work within the public service of British Columbia, I never thought of it as a hero's journey. My experience as a family counsellor, child protection Social Worker, and Team Leader in the Ministry of Social Services engaged me with helping others. For a while, I was the supervisor of Victoria Day Care Information Services. Day to day work in the field of abused and neglected children in the city's core neighbourhood exposed me to the underlying problems faced by so many troubled families.

The effects of poverty plagued many families. Often the problems that brought my clients through the doors, stemmed from the lack of adequate finances. The pressure on single-wage families, whether headed by one parent or two, was often manifested in abusive treatment of the children. I concluded that I was working at the discharge end of the social injustice pipe, and the solutions were higher in the social system.

In the period that I served as a family and child protection Social Worker, I volunteered as a union activist. When the government took over the agency and staff where I worked, I was the head of an independent union representing all the workers. The government had a legal obligation to honour the existing contract, even though it had not extended bargaining rights to its employees. That gave me a representational role negotiating for social service workers in the first round of bargaining between the BCGEU and the NDP government.

A few years later, the right-leaning Social Credit party returned to power. Despite its different ideological bent, the new government continued to productively negotiate with the union. However, at a time in the late 70s and early 80s inflation ran wild and the federal government introduced wage and price controls. A very different attitude showed up at the bargaining table. The government began a ten-year assault against the labour movement, especially the union that represented its own employees.

Throughout that time, I held most of the volunteer executive positions in the union. I became convinced that the union would have to strengthen the role of its representatives in the workplace. All the power and authority were concentrated in the headquarters operation, which showed up when the union needed to rely on the local leadership to conduct a province-wide strike. I advocated that the union become more democratic. Elected volunteers like me needed to take more responsibility.

Within the executive, I became an outspoken advocate for changing the constitution of the union to make the leadership more accountable to the membership. I became impatient with autocratic decision-making. The union needed the checks and balances that only strong elected leadership provides.

I did not realize the extent of my buried resentment at the Pope's autocratic and non-accountable behaviour. I honed in on people in authority behaving badly. Righting the power balance to give more say to the membership became a theme that ran through all my reforms in the union.

Over the course of many years as leader, I would mine nuggets of self-knowledge from the inner depths of my subconscious. The learning was slow and sometimes painful. At the heart of what I would learn was the spiritual lesson that there is no distinction between the outer world and the inner one.

After going through several rounds of bargaining that ended in strikes, I came to my first significant realization about myself. I had been blind to my compulsive behaviour patterns. What better occupation could I have chosen to repeatedly and legitimately challenge authority? The government was the ultimate authority. As the employer, they were the "immovable object" attracting the "irresistible force" of the employees' representative. As the head of the union, with a mandate from the members to make gains on their behalf, I repeatedly went into battle as the hero. I relished this role.

As a child, I struggled with my father over his misuse of authority. In my fifties, I came to realize that every few years I was repeatedly reenacting my power struggle with my father. Bargaining a large collective agreement covering thirty-five thousand people, is a major undertaking. There is extensive preparation, a great deal of ritual in the bargaining process, and many pieces that are important in themselves. I did not make the connection that I was doing my own psychological work until I had an awakening.

Four years after becoming president, I went through an experience that resulted in an explosive crisis. It was a clash of ideologies and power agendas at the highest political level in my province, and its impact resonated at my core.

A few months after Bill Vander Zalm was elected Premier of British Columbia, he invited me to a meeting that would determine both our fates. He told me that he wanted to eliminate the public sector in this province. He was going to start with the direct employees of government, and gradually expand out to include education and health. He would move as swiftly as he could, and only political expediency would slow him down. In an era dominated by the privatization agendas of Margaret Thatcher in Britain, Ronald Reagan in the United States, and Brian Mulroney in Canada, the ideology behind the Premier's grandiose scheme was familiar to me. I resolved to oppose his plan as forcefully as I could.

Philosophically I believe in the public good. I passionately believe that many things like health and protection of the environment should not be left to the profit motive. The elimination of the public service in government was a mad scheme, and I told the Premier that I would oppose him.

For the next nine months, I prodded my fellow union executives to help mount a campaign to protect public services. I traveled to every city and major community in British Columbia, a territory the size of Washington, Oregon and California combined. In every community, I met with Labour Councils, the local Chamber of Commerce and the municipal leaders. My plan to show the business leaders the amount of money that flowed into the local economy from the public service payroll, generated media coverage in each community I visited. In my presentation I showed each local group what was at stake from the loss of good paying jobs, and that they had evidence to oppose the privatization scheme.

At the end the province-wide campaign, the union went into bargaining for a collective agreement. Privatization was the centrepiece of the talks. The government's representatives opposed the union's position and we eventually reached an impasse. The members went on strike to support the union's negotiating position. One of the top mediators was invited into the dispute to assist both sides.

The bargaining sessions were intense. Feelings were running high on both sides. I was so intent about winning the day, when the mediator told me that our vice-president was hampering our discussions by his behaviour, instead of coaching him to act differently I just excluded him from the sessions. I offended him by exiling him from participating in the final hours of discussion.

When a settlement was finally reached, I felt triumphant. I brought the settlement to the bargaining committee. To my utter surprise, they seemed downcast and disgruntled. Their congratulations were half-hearted. I could not understand their tepid response after so long a struggle to stop the ravages of full-scale privatization. I could tell that the man I had excluded from the table had been working on them out of his hurt. When I finally asked the committee what was wrong, one of the women told me that they were disappointed with me. I had turned the negotiation into a one-person show. It was all me, and they had been left out. I had left them out. I was acting very differently from the way they were used to. Thus, they did not feel any ownership of the outcome. If the outcome was less than perfect, they did not feel it was their job to sell it to their members.

The membership of the union, however, voted overwhelmingly to approve the new contract, seeing the benefit it brought them. I regretted that I could not persuade the government to undo the privatizations that had already been pushed through. The Ministry of Transportation's Road and Bridge Maintenance crews had been handed over to individual contractors. The employees mostly went over to their new employers. Nonetheless, there was unhappiness among the crews, because we had promised we would do everything to keep them employed in government.

At the union's convention scheduled for a few months after the contract was ratified, I expected the members to be upbeat, sharing in the success of thwarting privatization of their work. Instead, there was a agitated mood. I had proposed a reorganization of the internal structure, in order to

117

accommodate the growth we were experiencing from organizing new members. Some of the executive would lose their positions, which fuelled some discontent.

When the time came to elect the officers, the mood had turned sour. Two members of the bargaining committee, including the one I had offended, announced that they would be running against me. I barely squeaked in, winning re-election by only twelve votes.

After the convention, I was despondent. I had poured my heart and energy into the campaign to frustrate the government agenda and succeeded. Yet, there did not seem to be any gratitude from the members. Even though I had won the election and would serve another term, I felt defeated.

I retreated to my Gulf Island cabin. For more than a week, I nursed my wounds and bordered on depression. Madeleine counselled me to be aware of my dreams, certain that I would receive guidance from my subconscious. That night I did have a vivid dream. My grandmother appeared to me as though she were in the room, telling me to pay attention to my heroes.

When I awoke, I told Madeleine about the dream and began to make a list of all the people I regarded as heroes. John and Bobby Kennedy, Martin Luther King, Tommy Douglas, David Suzuki were on my list. By the time I had completed my roster, there was no zing of recognition.

How did my grandmother's advice, to be aware of my heroes, resolve my dilemma? Perhaps I had not considered other heroes. I began to search my earliest childhood heroes. Radio shows from childhood were filled with heroes like Superman, Tom Mix and the Lone Ranger. As soon as the Lone Ranger came to mind, I knew I had struck gold. I recognized immediately that I was acting like the Lone Ranger. He was the hero in the white hat that rode into town on his white horse, Silver, to rescue the people from some dread crisis. He was strong and noble, and in the final scene, he would ride out of town to the grateful thanks of the crowd.

This was my myth; I was the Lone Hero. I saw in myself the hero in every story from the Odyssey to Star Wars.

I had incorporated the Lone Hero archetype as my own. The Lone Hero had been my personal myth since boyhood. Once triggered by hearing the premier's plan, everything I heard was interpreted through the myth. I was the actor, but it was the myth telling the story.

This accuracy of the insight hit me like a thunderclap. I had incorporated a mythic view, with myself as the hero, even before I went to school. Every time I was challenged, I would go into Lone Hero mode. When I reviewed my life, I realized all the times that the myth was at play. From my clashes with my father to tackling a provincial premier, the hero myth wrote the script of my story.

How could a myth be so influential, and I not know that it was working in me? Because I was on vacation, I had the leisure to contemplate my discovery. I had a story that enabled me to face the crises in my life. Whenever I was challenged, the myth turned on and ran on its own to the end of every story. The story I believed about myself was sitting in my subconscious, ready to become an action template.

My myth perpetuated my early life sense of isolation and separation. As a template, it gave me clues about how to act nobly in the face of any challenge. The Lone Hero needed no help to face the dragon. When it was operative, there was no place in my story for helpmates.

As I slowly examined all the implications of the Lone Ranger, I wondered whether I was stuck with that story for life. Clearly, it was not working in my present circumstances. If I internalized the story unconsciously, could I consciously change it? That summer on the shore of the Salish Sea, I began to systematically review other heroic myths to see if any of them fit. I wrote down the name of every mythic hero whenever one occurred to me. I described the attributes that I knew about that figure. I compared that story to the circumstances and values that I found in my life.

Two figures from mythology emerged repeatedly. The first was Merlyn; wizard, teacher and mentor of Arthur who would become king. I liked the wisdom Merlyn possessed and shared. He contributed to the future by training the future king. Despite its appeal, that image did not fully fit. Merlyn was a loner in the stories, and I had had enough of that characteristic.

The other hero story was King Arthur himself. I was attracted to the older Arthur who presided at the round table. He governed with compassion and wisdom. He was depicted as inspiring his knights to deeds of valour. Arthur commissioned the bravest knights to seek the Holy Grail. Here was my new myth. I thought about it, dreamed about it, wrote down the things I liked about it and then put it away.

When I returned to work, the new myth was not in my mind. Nonetheless, I was acting differently. I made different decisions. I found that those around me reacted differently as well. Things went smoothly. Discussions with senior advisors produced solid and effective plans. I seemed to be in a new flow: fewer struggles, more effectiveness.

As the days unfolded, I realized that what I was doing was not about me. I had shifted to make others the centre of my motivation. I was the leader of a large organization where my executives were all representatives of the membership. We had a collective wisdom role to play in protecting others and promoting their interests. That was not different from what it was before, but I was seeing it differently. For the next ten years, I was a different person. I was strong without being overbearing. I could be straight without worrying about what people would think about me. I accepted challenges without cringing, and if someone was right, I more readily admitted it and incorporated their viewpoint. I started to become wiser. Perhaps the wisdom of Merlyn was in me as well. My new story fit my situation, and the nobility of the Arthur figure was a good inspiration.

Why had I accepted the challenge of heading the union? At the time, I was very reluctant about becoming president. It would require me to give up my job as a Social Worker working with troubled families where I saw myself in a pastoral role, and immerse myself entirely in the field of labour relations. Moreover, I would need to take on responsibility for a large and complex organization with about thirty-six thousand members. The union was an entity with approximately forty staff representatives and an equal number of administrative personnel and there were two unions representing those staff. I would be responsible for a multi-million dollar budget.

Most troubling to me, I did not see myself reflected among the union leaders in that day. I had been on the executive for ten years by then, but I did not consider myself a professional labour relations practitioner. My self-image was not that of the tough labour union head.

I was reluctant to take on a high profile position that would require that I step into the archetype of the warrior. I had avoided the need to exercise my inner warrior. I preferred the quieter, gentler, voice of reason persona. If I were to become the union's leader, I would need to have the warrior's courage and strength.

I stepped up to the challenge of becoming president because I wanted to make a difference in the world. My formative experience with Fr. Berrigan had remained with me and shaped my motivation.

I would spend another ten years as president after that moment of enlightenment. I decided to use the power of my office to effect change. I would lead the union through deep transformational change. I recognized the opportunity not only to change my own union but also the broader labour movement. I faced the need to be clear about my motives and to have a clear moral compass to guide me in turbulent times.

I wanted to help my fellow workers. I wanted to do something for the marginalized in the workplace. Remembering the parents I dealt with as a social worker, I wanted to put more money and opportunity in their families. My first four years of navigating the waters of high stakes, power politics, I had developed the confidence to be myself and did not feel embarrassed by the fact that I needed to be powerful on behalf of others.

"Give priority to the needs of the poor." This was one concept that I remembered from Vatican II. In the workplace, women were the poor. They were not paid as well as men doing the same work. In any sector where women were the majority, that sector would be paid less than men. The glaring statistic fired my indignation. Most women worked under the poverty line. Older women lived in poverty because they had less access to pensions based on their employment years. I found that appalling. I was in a position to change that.

I persuaded the union to make a major shift, to reach out to the unorganized. Most male government employees in that time were relatively secure, and reasonably well paid. But not the women. They were certainly poor, second-class citizens, yet all around us were workers who needed what the union could provide.

I asked the union to adopt organizing as a key mode of work. We would re-structure the budget to put more resources into outreach. The target would be women. Women in credit unions and banks, in social services, and in health were all underpaid, compared to males in the public sector.

At the same time, women in the public service could not claim equal pay for work of equal value to men. I was able to persuade the first woman premier and her minister responsible for women's issues to negotiate a framework with the union to bring about pay equity for women in the provincial public service. We agreed that this would be outside of normal bargaining, and would not affect our collective agreement. They agreed.

I gave one of my staff who was an expert in the classifications, the mandate to work with the government to achieve a gender-neutral classification system. Although it took us several years to complete, we achieved pay equity. That accomplishment had enormous effects and was one of my greatest achievements.

The union targeted non-profit social services, health services, banks and credit unions, among other concentrations of women workers. I made a commitment to help the newly organized bargaining units to improve the lot of families. I saw that as a spiritual decision, putting resources to work to end poverty wherever I could.

During my years as president, I grew confident, drawing strength as I faced successive challenges. I was beginning to align my inner world to match my outer one. I brought inner integrity into all my public actions. My reputation for integrity was my most valued asset in the work I did. Integrity needed to be based on honest and trustworthy dealings with everyone.

I began to see the inner and outer integration as a spiritual value. The spiritual wisdom that emerged was rooted in the discovery of my myth. I realized that I needed congruence between the inner and the outer. There was no separation between what was right as a personal conviction and what was right as a public position. By believing that I could maintain consistency, that I could respect others and act from integrity, each moment presented the opportunity to be conscious of my greater self. I made the effort to consider each major decision in the context of what was the most compassionate course to follow.

Where I once believed that I could not act out of my inner values, I came to realize that created a contradiction between my inner compass and my outward behaviour. Healing the gap between what I thought was right and how I acted was most important. I was far less effective when I allowed the fear of how I would be judged to inhibit me from doing what I saw to be true to my inner lights. Sometimes my only choice was between the lesser of evils, but usually the greater good was available.

My path to growth had been painful, but it allowed me to access my innerscape. Awareness that consciousness co-creates the external circumstances continued to guide me. I was not an observer or an object being acted on. I was one with the creative energy of the cosmos, participating in the shaping of the world.

I became aware of how powerful my thoughts and intentions were. The enlightenment about the equal plane between my inner psyche and my external world became one of the pillars of my spirituality.

5

LIGHT FROM THE SKY

Every child needs to hear:
You came out of the energy
That gave birth to the Universe
It is your beginning.
You came out of the fire
That fashioned the galaxies:
It is alive within you

BRAIN SWIMME

When I realized that I had internalized a story that affected how I thought, I gained a new respect for story. Because of my belief that I was the hero of my story, I had been responding to the world out of that assumed archetype since childhood. My hero story shaped the way I saw the world, and determined how I reacted to it. What became clear was that my inner belief about my identity conditioned how I thought about the outer world.

With the discovery, I was able to consider whether that story still served me. The breakthrough into consciousness was enlivening. I saw that my inner and outer worlds were not separate but integrated. I had chosen to pursue conflict in the external world to enable me to resolve conflict that persisted within me. What better arena could I find to work out authority conflicts than in a forum where every two years I had to go up against the government, the archetype of authority, and test myself as the hero. It was a struggle driven by my ego, which itself was a construct of my mind.

I contemplated my new enlightenment. What could I learn from the power of the mind to create reality? Was I really in control of my thoughts and actions, or were there other outside filters that influenced how I thought? I began to wonder if my culture had a mythos. Did humanity have a collective myth? Was there a parallel story to my personal one buried in our collective subconscious?

In the early 90s, I was just becoming aware of the seriousness of the environmental crisis. Jack Munro, the Canadian head of the IWA – the International Woodworkers of America – was a fellow vice president of Federation of Labour. His union was coming under pressure for the practices of the companies logging the coast. There was growing controversy about the logging of pristine original growth forests on the West Coast. The environmental movement was mounting strong opposition to clear-cut logging and lobbying to ban logging in many pristine watersheds.

The largest company at that time, MacMillan Bloedel, was mounting a targeted defense of the company's activities. Jack invited me to take a helicopter tour of the wild West Coast of Vancouver Island, to see first hand what the company and his members were doing.

That trip had the opposite effect on me. I was shocked and disturbed by the destruction of huge tracts of ancient trees. My spirit recoiled at the sight of the giant Douglas fir trees lying dead on the ground. The attitude of the forester who was our guide was that the trees were resources for the company; they were there to be cut down so that humans could give them value. The loggers echoed this attitude. On that trip, I saw the heart of the crisis. Industry and workers saw the trees as things to be profited from, and the environmentalists saw them as living entities, with the right to protection. Instead of supporting the company and the loggers, I returned from that tour squarely on the side of nature.

Addressing a protest rally, 1997

As I was coming to grips with the environmental crisis, I realized how powerfully the Bible myth of Adam and Eve still influences modern thinking. The creation story from *Genesis* shaped the worldview of the West. What child has not heard of the Garden of Eden? In the Garden, God is pictured as giving Adam dominance over all creation. "God blessed them; and God said to them, 'Be fruitful and multiply, and fill the earth, and subdue it; and *rule over the fish of the sea and over the birds of the sky and over every living thing that moves on the earth.'*" (Gen. 1:28 New American Standard Version)

Two beliefs overlap and reinforce each other. The first is that the Bible is God speaking to humankind and therefore the text is a true guide. The second is that humans are separate from nature and were given the world as theirs to use as resources. Taken together, this story gives humans Divine permission to exploit the world.

By placing everything in the world at the disposal of humans, Christianity has fostered the attitudes that have led to the environmental crisis of today. St. Augustine in the fifth century of the Common Era used the Adam and Eve story to declare the world sinful. John Locke in the seventeenth century used the literal interpretation of the myth to justify the private ownership of property. The church has used the literal understanding of the creation story to support the condemnation of Galileo and the dismissal of Darwin. The literal reading of *Genesis* has pitted religion against science for several hundred years. Believing the mandate in the Garden to be true, Christianity has embedded its interpretation of *Genesis* into the consciousness of the West. It has influenced the development of Capitalism and Liberalism in Europe and its colonies. The representatives of the forestry companies and their loggers believed that they were divinely sanctioned to use the environment for their benefit.

I thought about the biblical story of creation the evening I first heard Dr. Brian Swimme describe the discoveries scientists had recently made about the universe. I was hearing a new story, one that did not yet make sense to me.

Swimme was introduced as a cosmologist. I did not really know what a scientific cosmologist was, although I had studied cosmology in philosophy classes in the Seminary. I knew that cosmology played a very large part in shaping the worldview of the authors of the Bible. In biblical times, the assumptions everyone made about the universe, showed up in the way they described the world. The earth was thought to be small and flat. The heavens were a solid dome over the Earth, not too far above the mountains. In his talk, the young

Californian described a very different vision of the universe. He spoke eloquently and enthusiastically about the wonders that scientists had uncovered as they studied the evidence of the Big Bang.

Swimme brought the cosmic origin alive. I found his excitement about the new discovery was contagious. While he was talking about the new cosmology, I was remembering what I knew of the ancient one. He commented that everyone who had ever lived assumed that the universe had always been like we see it now. The Bible authors believed that the world was created as is by God. The creation story inferred that it was a perfect paradise in the beginning but that humans were responsible for its degradation.

Secular scientists assumed that the universe was eternal, and unchanging and for the most of Western history, humans accepted that story. Swimme recalled that Albert Einstein began to explore light, time and space. Einstein concluded that movement of light indicated that the universe should be expanding. The American astronomer Edwin Hubble showed Einstein that the universe was expanding in every direction. If that is so, he concluded, they must have a common starting place. In the early twentieth century, Einstein declared that the universe began from a single energy event, but at that time there was no way to prove his theory.

Swimme told his audience that in the mid-sixties, two scientists at Bell Laboratories in New Jersey accidentally discovered evidence that confirmed Einstein's theory about the origin of the universe. Arno Penzias and Robert W. Wilson found static coming from everywhere in the universe. They won the Nobel Prize in Physics in 1978 by realizing that they were observing the remnants of the birth of the universe. The radiation they discovered was the remnant of the event that Einstein had described. All previous assumptions about the nature of the cosmos were erased by this discovery.

The National Aeronautics and Space Administration (NASA) became very curious about the discovery of what came to be called the Cosmic Microwave Background (CMB). The scientists set out to explore the evidence and in 1989, NASA launched a probe dubbed the Cosmic Background Explorer or COBE. The satellite searched the heavens for traces of the radiation suspected to come from the originating event. When the information from COBE was analyzed, NASA released the images. The image turned out to be the most important image in human history. It changed the way humanity would think about the universe and everything in it. The image confirmed the universe had a beginning and that, from the outset, it was capable of evolving. NASA's work set off the development of a new cosmology that would eclipse all previous understandings of the universe.

The image (Figure 1) provided conclusive evidence for the Big Bang. American scientists were then convinced of the birth of the universe. The NASA media release said:

> In essence, the satellite, launched in November 1989, has peered back in time to detect the now faint whispers of the Big Bang that is widely believed to have started the expansion of the universe about 15 billion years ago. "What we've done is to measure the microwave radiation that comes to us almost equally from every direction and that is thought to be the primary remnant of the Big Bang," said [Dr. John] Mather.

Figure 1: Cosmic Microwave Background (NASA)

In his talk that evening, Brian Swimme painted a picture of a startling change in humanity's understanding of the origin of the cosmos. The emerging new concepts shook my understanding of the universe to my core.

I did not know it at the time, but Swimme was opening a door to spirituality for me. I would need several more years and a lot more study to integrate what I heard that night, but the new story of the cosmic origins was so new and different, that it completely transformed my understanding of reality.

Thomas Berry perceived the continuing energy event as both spiritual and material. He was Swimme's mentor, and he offered a profoundly spiritual understanding of the originating event. Together, they introduced me to a transforming understanding of the origin and nature of the cosmos. The scope and depth of the new perspective shifted my consciousness completely reorienting my psychic compass.

The image from NASA meant that everything that is now in the universe arose from that initial flaring of energy. I began to understand that the cosmos is evolutionary, developing one stage at a time over time. It is a unitary entity. It is acting.

Fr. Berry described the amazing evolutionary process of cosmogenesis. The revolutionary idea is that the universe is fully responsible for its own generation. Gosmogenesis is the name of the discovery that the universe is self-generating. It is producing its own unfolding from within its internal dynamic. No external force or influence is possible. Everything in the universe emerges out of it. There is no outside or before.

The starting thermonuclear eruption created the elementary particles that began a chain reaction of development. In the beginning, every particle is exposed to every other particle setting up a field of connection where everything is in unity. The incipient universe contained all the seeds that would flower over time to become this earth, the

Milky Way Galaxy, and all the billions of galaxies and billions of stars in every galaxy. The universe, emerging from the scattered waves of energy we see in Figure 1 evolves into the far-flung array of stars and galaxies that are now everywhere.

I paid close attention to the parallels between the creative process of the universe's unfolding from within its essence and the power of my consciousness to create my reality. Berry used the phrase "the new story" to describe the flowing narrative of the unfolding universe. I identified with the idea of a new story as part of the process of continuing from story to story. I was especially interested that a priest would be so comfortable with new developments replacing the older story that has been so formative of Western thinking. The idea of story, he said, conveys the notion of a single ongoing narrative that is not finished. Surprising me by his openness to a scientific way of understanding the unfolding cosmos, Berry relied on the new information to augment the now ancient biblical way of describing the beginning.

I was attracted to the idea of story. It would be easy to get lost in the technical science. The information about the emerging understanding is scientific, but the meaning of the information is universally accessible. Repeatedly I too had been evolving. Each turn in the path was an opportunity to grow. Growth was emerging from my innermost being, and was continually taking me into new territory.

Like Teilhard de Chardin, who many years ago opened my eyes to the depth of spiritual fire in the cosmos, Berry's inspired writings on the emergence of the conscious spiritual energy provided insights into the meaning of ongoing creativity.

As I kept learning more about the findings of the cosmologists, I would excitedly tell my friends about it, like the latest installment of a good serial.

There are many reasons why I was so excited about the new story. The first is that it joins science and spirit. Now the best scientists sound like mystics. The scientific visionaries who have gone beyond the paradigm of a material cosmos describe energy as conscious and spirit filled.

In the past, most scientists shied away from the non-material. On the other hand, theologians are so deeply rooted in their religious tradition that they were blind to the more wondrous implications of the information coming from science. I welcomed the scientific insights into the way the universe is. We cannot speak about the nature of the universe now without including spirit, meaning and purpose.

Because of science, humanity's perception of the universe has changed completely. We are now in a time of transition. The worldview that emerged from the materialistic cosmology still holds sway over our imaginations. The new story is directing us away from a mechanistic view of the universe. I hope that the earth and the environment will benefit from this turning as we reject the flawed materialistic belief about the world. It is urgent that we embrace the implication of a conscious cosmos, and change our destructive ways of living on earth.

If our previous fundamental assumptions about the nature of the universe were wrong, than every conclusion we drew from those assumption would be flawed. Certainly, the cosmology that was prevalent when religions were developed proved false. The replacement assumption, namely that of the material, mechanical universe, is now shown to be equally flawed. Unravelling the grip of the materialistic worldview will be a gargantuan task. Yet, for the sake of humanity and the planet, we must rapidly change our minds.

What is emerging has huge spiritual implications. It has changed my sense of where I come from, who I am, and my destiny in the future. I am amazed that more is not being made of it. You and I originate in the universe. We are part of a single whole. The universe is not dead matter, but a living consciousness.

Humanity is being shown a self-generating universe, one that is a single energy event. Everything that has ever existed is part of the evolutionary dynamic of the cosmos. I now see that at our most fundamental level, that we share identity with all other creatures in nature. We are united and one.

How can we despoil our world for selfish gain when we know that we are contaminating parts of ourselves? It is a violation of our very nature to harm the natural world.

I have concluded that I am in the universe to continue and to foster the development of the unfolding earth. My deepest nature wants to be aligned with whatever enhances the life on earth. The clearer I get about my oneness with the earth and with all creation, the more I know myself. I experience myself with an urgent sense of responsibility to stop the destruction. At the same time, I am at peace, knowing that I am of the universe, and one with the All.

From what I have learned of our cosmic origins, the universe is constantly creating the present moment. The expansion of time/space is progressing, and regenerating one moment at a time. This is an enormous spiritual lesson. The only time is now. This is the only time there is, and in it is the entire evolution from the beginning of the Big Bang, 13.7 billion years ago.

While I have shifted to accept that everything is evolving, changing, developing, the entire evolutionary history is pointed at this present moment. Now, therefore, is the most significant point in time/space. What an auspicious moment to be alive.

Because this is the culmination of cosmic history, it is the fruition of the cosmogenesis. The universe has evolved to this moment. While there is a great deal of chance, there is no sense of accident. The universe is directing evolution. I ask myself, why am I in this moment? Everything I do comes from how I understand the answer.

The best new science and the best of the spiritual wisdom of the ages suggests that you and I are in this moment to contribute what only we can add to the matrix. We come out of the universe to play a role in the unfolding of the universe. This perspective riveted me. This is the opposite of meaninglessness. I come forth at this precise moment to contribute my unique gifts to the great unfolding.

The cosmos is a matrix from which everything flows. Those describing the cosmos could be speaking of a "thou" rather than an "it." I regard the matrix with reverence. I see in it the sacred nature of the Great Mother. I espouse the emerging perception that the cosmos is a living entity.

To me, the universe is a radiant, expanding reality. I see myself in it and of it. The compelling power of this discovery has galvanized my identification with the sacred nature of everything. I abandoned the religious orientation that came from Christianity. And for more than twenty years, I searched for the key to a new spiritual understanding. With the new story, the biblical story has been augmented by new revelation. I was never comfortable accepting the materialistic view. With the emerging worldview, an entirely different template is now available. The scientific information provided by NASA and the cosmologists has given me the universe's self-understanding. The profoundly spiritual discovery for me is in the sense of who I am and where I come from.

I now feel solidly anchored as part of the unfolding cosmos. My renewed spirituality requires that I see that this moment cooking since the beginning of time. As a result, I believe that I am in this time and this place in order to play a specific role in the continuing unfolding of the cosmos. I have been developing a greater self-awareness, so that I am more conscious of what I am bringing into the creative process.

What I bring into this moment is a manifestation of cosmic intention. I have come to see that the increase of my consciousness is connected to an unfolding awareness within the cosmos. If the universe is truly one, then my consciousness and the universe are also one. Could it be that my questions are the universe exploring itself?

The questions I have about the environment, the future health of the planet, and aboriginal wisdom that comes from an ancient connection to nature, come together. My thirst for social justice, to see an end to abject poverty, to the equal distribution of clean water, for maternal health, and an end to high infant mortality is connected to my sense of responsibility to the well-being of the whole of humanity. I yearn for an end to war and the causes of war. Each new inquiry leads to increasing consciousness, which in turn leads to greater curiosity about how to make the world function better. The resulting insights plunge me deeply into mystery.

Consciousness, both my own and the collective experience, is key to the emerging view of the cosmos. Consciousness is analogous to the background radiation that originates from the Big Bang. It shows up as a quality in everything at its deepest level. Consciousness has been described as the ability to experience. Researchers have discovered that it is present at the most minute quantum level. Consciousness, so prized by spiritual seers throughout history, is turning out to be a fundamental property of the cosmos.

The mystery and awe increases as the scientists tell us that the universe itself is determining the rate of expansion of the elements forged in the original gush of energy. The relationship and ratios determined in the first instant of the emergence of cosmic energy indicates that the universe chose how it would expand. The rate of expansion determined the formation of galaxies, which in turn continue to generate new stars in the hundreds of billions. The evidence from Hubble points to the observation that this is an ongoing process.

A flood of investigations and discoveries has yielded insights into the properties of the heavens. These revelations are profoundly relevant. I am of the earth and standing in a new and more solid orientation to the cosmic whole. What shines out from all the work done on the new story is that everything in the universe is interconnected. No place is isolated from the whole. There is growing evidence that no element or particle exists disconnected from all other matter. Indeed, the evidence is now convincing that the universe is generating itself from the single source, and that the energy that gave rise to the first galaxy is still animating life on earth today. Everything that is participates in a single web of being. All the dazzling diversity of minerals, animals and plants that make up the earth arises out of earth. As a member of the earth community of life, I am of the universe and an integral part of a cosmic whole.

The mystery grows more numinous. The compelling force of these discoveries reverberates in me at the soul level. I know instinctively that the breakthroughs in the last quarter century have revolutionized my sense of place. The assumptions that had been guiding humanity's understanding of the universe, the belief that it was lifeless and meaningless, have been set aside to make room for an entirely different understanding. In place of the static view, there is a growing sense of a living and dynamic integrated entity that is acting to achieve its own unfolding.

The dynamic and complex evolution of the universe, from a cauldron of thermal energy led to the billions of galaxies and trillions of stars. As I come to appreciate where I fit in this story, I am awakened to a profound sense of wonder and awe.

Light From The Sky

6

THE CALL OF THE WILD

The most beautiful thing we can experience is the
mysterious. It is the source of all true art and all science.
He to whom this emotion is a stranger, who can no
longer pause to wonder and stand rapt in awe, is as
good as dead: his eyes are closed.

ALBERT EINSTEIN

I live in Victoria now, on the shores of the Salish
Sea in British Columbia. From my front windows, I
look across the Strait of Juan de Fuca at the snow-
capped Olympic Mountains in the state of
Washington. The city was a fur-trading outpost
and a staging place for the Cariboo gold rush.
Despite being one of the oldest cities on the West
Coast, Victoria has retained beauty and charm. In
less than a half hour's drive, I can be in a pastoral
countryside, and an hour's travel brings me into
forest and the foothills of the mountains. Whether I
am by the open sea or in the ancient forest, I am
conscious of my connection to the natural world.

Ever since I first settled here, I have been aware that First Nations communities dot the shores and forests. I have been enriched by aboriginal culture and art, reminding me that I have come to this place that has been occupied for thousands of years by people indigenous to this place.

The stunning beauty of the environment keeps me conscious of my close connection to nature. Though I live in the city, every day I see the migrating sea birds, the whales and eagles.

I have grown in my concern about what we are doing to our fragile planet. I worry that it may be too late to restore the balance and the environmental crisis has become a profound spiritual crisis for me.

On a rainy November day several years ago, I gathered with a group of men from a spirituality circle that I had been facilitating for many years. Deep in the rainforest of Canada's Pacific Northwest, fifteen of us had come to explore how we could reconnect with nature. Some of us were from urban centres, others from rural communities. At that time, I lived in a rural setting on a coastal island. Our purpose for the gathering was the common interest to become more connected with nature. We acknowledged that the human-dominated life patterns had replaced or obscured the rhythms of nature in our awareness. We had become disconnected from Earth. We acknowledged that we had become reliant on the built environment at the expense of our primal relationship to the natural world. We were asking ourselves if we had all traded spiritual well-being for material comfort. We acknowledged that we were feeling out of harmony within ourselves and isolated from the natural world. That weekend we wanted to revive our deep connection to the wild.

The first night of our gathering, an elder from a local indigenous community had reminded us that aboriginal people had prospered in that land. They knew the cycles of nature, when and where to harvest the abundant plant and marine life. Locally abundant foods once could feed an entire village when harvested with respect and understanding of the recurring cycles of growth and migration. He told us that among the First Nations there is an expression of acknowledgment: "All my relations." The concept was not limited to family. The affirmation recognized kinship of all the elements of nature as well as the human presence. The worldview of the aboriginal people encompassed everything that supported life. Even the rocks were called the 'grandmothers' because they contained the wisdom of the ages. He spoke of these relationships fondly as an expression of connection with all that is.

Living in harmony with the natural world was central to the elder's teaching. This tenet was the heart of the way First Peoples around the globe live and practice their core values. From the tip of Peru to the Arctic tundra, indigenous people have a relationship with the world that sustains them. Aboriginal people do not think of themselves as separate from land or sea.

When I was head of the union, the provincial and federal governments appointed me as a labour representative to the Treaty Negotiation Advisory Committee (TNAC). The committee, composed of business, government, labour and environmental leaders, had the responsibility to advise government about how treaty proposals would affect various interests in the province.

During our deliberations, I witnessed the clash between descendents of European colonizers and BC's First Nations. As the committee reviewed the impact of future treaties on fish, mining and forestry, corporate sector representatives refused to accept any claim that the First Peoples had to the wealth of the land. They denied that the First Peoples had any claim to the land they had inhabited for thousands of years. The people who now controlled the logging and fishing industries, did everything they could to block the First Nations from regaining their rights to prosperity.

I had never witnessed such raw racism since I was involved in the Civil Rights struggle in the southern United States. For thousands of years, First Nations lived off their harvest of salmon and shellfish. They now were denied the right to catch fish in their traditional territories for food and ceremony. As though they were invisible, aboriginal people were expected to prove that they had a right to exist to settlers who had moved into their traditional territories.

I was just discovering my place in the cosmos. The emerging thinking was that everything and everyone on the earth had a common origin in the evolution of the planet. We are all one. The deeply spiritual implication of our oneness was beginning to sink in.

I had been raised to trust that my senses were an accurate reflection of the world. I was just then beginning to challenge the fact that my senses were a reliable representation of the reality all around me. Since the early part of the twentieth century, quantum physicists had been saying that the subatomic world was strangely dissimilar from the world we perceive. The COBE probe was then newly confirming that the vast universe is primarily energy. What we see is not solid, neither at the microscopic level nor in the macro scale. The scattered galaxies and stars in the night sky are a template for the atomic and molecular pattern below the visible scale. I did not understand why we do not perceive energy or why human senses mask the fact that the universe is alive with consciousness and spirit. The new discoveries tell us that this was indeed the case.

I was coming to comprehend that it is necessary to understand how essentially One we are with the entire universe. We cannot look at trees and salmon as merely resources there for our use. Our consciousness has to come into alignment with the reality of the universe.

The Maya of Middle America see themselves as connected to the heart of the sky and the heart of the earth. Their cosmology is holistic and their worldview integrates humans and nature. The

Maya have endured in the face of overwhelming pressure to conform to western values by holding to their cosmology and their worldview. Their sense of unity with the world was alien to the European settlers who came to the new world and attempted to "civilize" them.[5]

The nature-based spirituality of the Maya is a clue to what is possible as we struggle to reclaim our relationship to nature. If we examine the ways that our contemporary society's views differ from the views of the First Peoples, we can pinpoint where they diverge. The original people on this land knew they depended on the fish, the caribou, or the buffalo for their sustenance and survival. They valued the diversity of plant life and the animals they lived with. They drew on these for food and medicinal healing and they did so with respect. Over thousands of years, they developed a balanced relationship with the animals, plants, of land and the sea. Out of this age-old realization of the interdependence of human with nature, First Peoples evolved a worldview that sustained them.

---

[5] Dr. Robin June Hood, *A Curriculum of Place and Respect: Towards an Understanding of Contemporary Mayan Education*, University of Victoria, (unpublished doctoral thesis).

The local First Nations hold nature with reverence. For them, the human presence in the world is one with the whole, and not experienced as separated from the environment. The people who first inhabited the wild places saw themselves as essential to the interplay of elements. I now realize how powerful a role cosmology plays in the way everyone sees and reacts to the world.

Until recently, our society has shown little sign of challenging its worldview. What is changing now is the growing number of people who want to take part in what Joanna Macy calls 'the Great Turning'. The numbers of people who are tapping into the spirituality of the earth continues to grow. We are witnessing one of the greatest transformations in thinking in centuries.

In the lodge among the giant trees in the Sooke hills, the elder used stories and parables to illustrated his teachings and life lessons. The stories had come down by word of mouth from generation to generation. As he offered us his wisdom, I sat in the circle, mesmerized by the fire that blazed in the huge stone fireplace. The flames carried my imagination beyond the large hall into far-flung communities in the wilderness. In my mind, I stood beside hunters and fishers dwelling in harmony with their surroundings.

"How did we fall out of connection with nature?" one man in the circle asked. Was it really progress to wind up alienated from the natural world? Our generation, as so many before us, was formed by a worldview that placed no value on the environment or the natural world. The worldview we inherited thought that the material world had no inherent value, no spirit, and no importance except as resource for human needs. Like the ancient worldview before it, the materialist view placed humans at the top of pyramid. We have been educated to take for granted that everything is at our disposal. Twenty-one centuries of Western thinking had cemented our view.

I acknowledged that for much of my life I had taken the environment for granted. It was merely there to be used: resources to be exploited. Indeed, I once thought there was nothing to be learned from a lifeless cosmos.

Deep among towering trees in the rain forest, the men who had gathered round the fire agreed that we were impoverished by our separation from a deep connection to the earth. We mused about how the human community had changed. In the beginning, people had depended on nature and lived in harmony with the environment, respecting the other members of the earth community as fellow creatures. One man in the group spoke about the possibility that humanity could destroy life on earth. He sounded the alarm about the dangers of how far we have already strained the quality of environmental health. He warned us that we were causing the greatest eradication of species since the extinction of the dinosaurs, sixty-five million years ago. He pointed out that we were doing this by the way we treated the earth's essential elements – air, water and soil. He asked if any of us could show any evidence that humans have benefited any other species on earth beside themselves.

The scope and scale of human pillaging of the earth is so huge that my mind could not cope with the magnitude of the issue. I heard stories of how many trees are being cut down each day in Africa or South America. In my own region, I have seen truckloads of ancient trees cut down and destined for shipment to other parts of the world.

A news report recently told of whales gone missing from the local pods. Seven to ten whales are presumed to have starved to death. Was there a connection between the pollution of the ocean and the loss of the whales? Is the disappearance of salmon from our waters the result of bad aquaculture management, logging or global warming?

A headline from a few years ago baldly stated that a study from the US concluded that only 10% of the ocean's fish remain. One fisherman in the group told us that the oceans are dying because of human abuse, and yet we resist taking the necessary steps to conserve and preserve them. Humans refuse to accept the direct connection between the decline in the life systems of our planet and our behaviour. How am I connected to the die-off of salmon and the death of the whales? And how am I affecting the bears and eagles that rely on those fish for their diets?

This was not a new awareness. I began feeling the plight of the earth around the time that I left the priesthood and returned to British Columbia from Texas. The experience of abandoning the clergy, rejecting my religion, and leaving the place where I was known and honoured triggered a profound sense of loss. When I came to my new home in Victoria, I felt little connection to the place. I was longing for somewhere else. The dissonance I felt permeated everything in my life. My new marriage, my work, my relationship with my mother and father in New York, even my friends from the Paulist Fathers and from Austin were all affected. I looked at life through the prism of loss, resentment and loneliness. I had never before felt such a strong sense of estrangement. The suffering environment became a symbol for my inner state of being.

I heard Joanna Macy speak when I was the Executive Director at a retreat centre called The Haven. Joanna made an impression on me when she advised the people on retreat with her, not to quell the anguish and pain they felt at what is happening to the natural world. If we do, she said, we dull ourselves to being in the reality. We cannot participate in the Great Turning unless we are fully aware and connected to the plight of the natural world.

Three extraordinary First Nations leaders stand out as friends and teachers. Each taught me about being a leader who integrated place, environment, and a determination for justice – Joe Gosnell, Chief of the Nisga'a Nation, Joe Mathias, Chief of the Squamish Nation, and George Watts, Chief of the Nuu-chah-nulth and founder of the Nuu-chah-nulth Tribal Council. I knew each of the Chiefs from three quite different Nations. Each held a conviction that their people could come into harmony with the society that had come to settle in their territories, provided that their fundamental rights were acknowledged. Each was a traditional leader in the tribal lineage of their own First Nation, each was a spiritual person deeply connected to the earth.

Chief Joe Gosnell, the heredity leader of the Nisga'a people in the rugged Nass River valley in northern British Columbia invited me to his home village. On a walk, he pointed to a mountain near his home and told me that he derived his identity from that mountain. I saw a profound relationship between man and place. His spiritual strength was rooted in the place where his people have lived for ten thousand years. This was one of the clearest examples of strong connection between people and the natural world. What I took away from my relationship with Chief Gosnell was that aboriginal spirituality is imbedded in nature and in place. He showed me that we cannot stand apart from nature and look at it as though it is different from us. When humans study nature, they are within the context rather than apart from it. I remembered that quantum mechanics long ago proved that the observer is part of the field of study. Contemporary cosmology reinforces that we are within the whole.

Humanity is a product of the evolving universe. There is no outside from which to study nature. Indigenous people have always known this.

The limitation of the Western religious tradition was that it taught that humans were only passing through this world. Religious thinkers did not know in the second or third centuries that we are of the universe. They projected that to attain life meant to leave the earth for a heaven in the sky. Many religious scholars, like Mary Ellen Tucker, are embracing the principle that we have a radical responsibility for the earth.

The most empirical study of cosmology is concluding that the energy that gives rise to all material in the universe is conscious, and has been from the first instant of its manifestation. With the presence of consciousness comes what we have called spirit. Consequently, human spirituality must be rooted in the earth. I know my spirituality through my bodily senses. I cannot be spiritual in my head alone. I cannot care for the whales if I only look at them as different, as though they are separate from me. I am one with the whales in one complex fabric, because we are the earth community. Spirituality that is not grounded in the stuff of the Earth is ephemeral and unengaged.

Contemporary science shows us we are produced by the slow evolution over billions of years. Knowing that takes away any temptation to be haughty, or to remain apart from the flow of energy as it pushes forward to be the universe moving to its completion.

Consciousness of place is key to indigenous spirituality. Consciousness is the source of human ability to perceive the more-than-material nature of the world in which we live. Consciousness is the element of experience that the Buddha identified as enlightenment. Consciousness was the illumination that transformed my subconscious mythology into a more relevant one. Consciousness is a constituent of everything in the universe. The energy that brought the cosmos into what we know it to be is conscious.

Some time after I retired from the union, I began to work with men who wanted to explore spirituality in their lives. We met in a circle every Wednesday evening. A circle is a very powerful setting for people to be part of, because it is a container and distributor of energy. The Wednesday Spirituality group is still meeting more than ten years after it started. At the outset, we agreed to some guidelines that have made the setting a safe one within which to share deep thoughts. We agreed that we met to explore spirituality, and that spirit showed up in respect. We would treat each other with respect. We would listen with a full concentration whenever anyone else was speaking. We would not interrupt, contradict, or act as though we had a better idea or understood something better than anyone else. In that atmosphere, thoughts and reflections are best expressed in the first person, from one's own experience. Someone's experience cannot be contradicted. If they share what is in their heart, they are offering gold.

In that spirit of respect, some profound sharings have taken place. Men reached into their depths to share, be heard and be healed. The circle of men created a way of being together. When someone new joined the circle, they were asked if they would subscribe to the agreements of the group. The circle modeled the behaviour that had become characteristic of the group. The safe environment allowed what was inner to come to the fore. I was always amazed at how deep men would go in that environment.

Conscious awareness occurs in an environment of safety, and it is enhanced when I experience acceptance. The bridge between heart and mind, between inner and outer is supported in the circle when people commit to being together with respect. I have a suspicion that the qualities that were accessed in the circle, although rare in our interactions with one another, make a profound difference to our experience. The circle was a place of intention, and a place defined by ritual. We began each evening by experiencing a few minutes in silence, shedding the stresses of our day, and then we would go round the circle, expressing gratitude for something in our lives. We concluded the evening by another round in which an appreciation was expressed for someone or something that happened in the circle.

I experienced the circle as spiritual. The energy of the circle was palpable to everyone who shared in the circle experience. The qualities of respectfully sharing allow what is hidden to come forward. The intention to attend to each other with respect and interest allows the depth of the other to come forth and meet us across the bridge of open heartedness. In the connection our attention goes forth and embraces the spirit of the person speaking as though that was the most important thing we could do at that moment. The tangible experience of unity and caring fostered peace and healing.

I noted that the aboriginal people do all their significant deliberations in a circle. According to the Arthurian legend, Arthur met with his knights around a circular table that communicated a sense of equality with the king to all. In the spirit of unity that the circle conveys, Arthur sent his companions on their quests from the round table. The circle is the traditional symbol of spirit.

I now believe that consciousness is the portal to spirituality. Consciousness is a state that can be developed in everyone. In my development, my greatest impetus to consciousness was meditation. The form I chose was Transcendental Meditation taught by Maharishi Mahesh Yogi.

Once I accepted that the universe is unfolding with consciousness, I realized that there is purposefulness in the evolutionary chaos, and the universe is selecting the path toward its ultimate direction. Tillard de Chardin called that the Omega Point which is calling the universe forward.

In the energy of the circle, which is the energy of this place and this time, we are replicating the shape of the galaxies and the form of the creation of the stars. It takes an open heart to see the spiritual significance in symbols, and to know that the symbols lead us into the mystery of cosmic self-creation.

The journey to spirit is a journey to mystery. Spirit is not found in the concrete, although we discover it through our earthly bodies. Peter Russell, a theoretical physicist and mystic, sees the evidence of spirit at the inception of the universe in the identification of spirit and light. They share the same properties, he says, and both are present in the tumult of the cauldron of elements that produce the emerging cosmos[6]. I am attracted to the likening of consciousness and light in the universe at the metaphoric and transcendental level of cosmic unfolding.

The universe that is revealing itself to us in the evidence of the new cosmos is so much more wonderful than anything that even the most advanced seers perceived. It is not beyond our understanding. To the contrary, it invites us to enter the mystery and imbibe the majesty of its nature. The cosmos is not small in size, and it is beyond reckoning in its full dimension. We are likely to find ourselves in rapture of its dimensions for ages to come.

And, in both a scientific and poetic sense, we are the universe. The universe is in us, in the sense that

---

[6] Peter Russell, *From Science to God, The Mystery of Consciousness and the Meaning of Light,* Novato, California New World Library, 2003.

we manifest it in all its majesty. We are the universe reflecting on itself, as we explore the ramifications of what it is revealing.

The cosmic revolution that began with the image of the cosmic radiation is only just revealing its implications. Collectively, we are only starting to grasp the meaning of what we are being shown. With each new insight, we are being challenged to abandon all those flawed concepts that are unworthy of the universe that is showing itself to us.

I am struggling to integrate the knowledge that is coming at a prodigious rate, the expansion of my consciousness that is being generated by the new information and the insights that accompany each new discovery, and to keep all of that in the context of spirit and humility. The exciting aspect of this moment is that we are able to participate in the exploration of the beginning of this new phase in cosmic evolution.

7

LIFE AND DEATH IN THE UNFOLDING COSMOS

Tell me, what else should I have done?
Doesn't everything die at last and too soon?
Tell me, what is it you plan to do
With your one wild and precious life?

MARY OLIVER

My experience of the death of my father and mother happened at a time before I was fully awake to my emotional life. That did not mute the pain I felt at their loss. Each of those deaths pushed me toward the brink of my mortality. Each was a catastrophic loss. I was an only child, and after my parents' death, I felt like an orphan.

I was under forty when my mother died. She appeared to have a stroke, rapidly lost her capacity to speak, and finally the use of her mind. She was admitted to a nursing home in Southampton with what turned out to be cancer of the brain. Her deterioration occurred in eight months. I had to travel across the continent to visit her. I drove to see her five times during her decline, and the visits left me full of dread and anguish. Madeleine usually accompanied me on these visits. On one visit, when we arrived at the care home, my mother had lost her ability to speak. However, when she noticed Madeleine, she glared at her with unvarnished hatred. I could only assume that her early opinion that Madeleine was responsible for my leaving the priesthood and moving to the west coast had surfaced with blame and resentment. I would have defended my wife from my mother, but Madeleine recoiled from the look, and I knew she had suffered from it.

I was deeply conflicted. I felt compassion for my mother and her condition. I strongly wanted to bring her to Victoria so that I could comfort her and visit her more often. Her doctor did not want her moved. After her death, the doctor revealed that the cause of death was cancer of the brain. I did not know the extent of her suffering for it was not on the outside. She was not in pain, but she gradually lost conscious connection to the world around her.

I distanced myself from feeling the effect of my mother's death. I was numb to the loss. It took many years and inner struggle before I was able to fully mourn her passing. I loved her and missed her, and at the same time, I resented the way she could use her emotions to control mine.

When Madeleine was diagnosed with an incurable cancer, it was twenty years after my mother's death. I knew what the death of loved ones felt like. I anticipated the pain of loss. The prospect of Madeleine's death awakened in me the traumatic experiences of childhood abandonment, and these early life experiences were lodged in my primitive brain. Even though I have now cleared the memory out of my muscles where it had blocked the free flow of my energy, my reptilian brain was reacting to the prospect of loss and reading it as abandonment.

Five years passed from Madeleine's initial diagnosis to a time when the lymphoma symptoms started being debilitating. In the late nineties, tumors showed up throughout her body, and her health began to fail in other ways.

Madeleine had strong views about the available options for cancer patients. She called the treatments, "cut, burn or poison". She did not want to participate in any of them, especially since in her case there was no clear likelihood they would cure the cancer. She was not interested in simply prolonging her life in a state of debilitation. I was not as sanguine about her not availing herself of the best of medical science, but I could not prevail over her conviction about how to care for herself.

She thought that there might be help in an energy treatment that was described in a book on alternative treatments. We invested in a light beam generator from the United States, and I underwrote the cost of a local energy medicine practitioner to learn the protocols for using it effectively. To my amazement, over the course of four months, the tumors shrunk as the woman applied the light beam in conjunction with lymph massage.

I had once thought that Madeleine would not outlive the year and was making plans to step down from the presidency of the union. She was adamant that as long as there were signs of improvement, I continue my job. A friend of hers, who is a trained nurse, came from Saskatoon to Victoria to be with her. Mary Maxwell came in every day for months to look after her practical needs. Madeleine's cancer seemed to be going into remission. Nonetheless, I told the union I would not be seeking re-election for another term.

After a heartwarming send off at the union's convention, I shifted my energy from the broad stage of union leadership to the very specific stage of caring for one other person. The change was more difficult than I suspected. For many years, I had maintained an apartment in Vancouver, close to the union's headquarters. I needed to pack up my office and my apartment and relocate to our home in Victoria.

Madeleine often described our living arrangement as ideal for a middle-years marriage. I was free to devote all my energy to my work, without needing to attend to anyone else's needs or schedule. For Madeleine, the quiet of an undisturbed environment at home allowed her to paint and teach.

She had adopted the painting of mandalas as her primary art form and spiritual practice. After returning to art school in the early eighties, she studied with Jack Wise, a well-known West Cost painter. Jack had adapted the Tibetan Buddhist mandala by substituting inner psychological symbols for the religious iconography of Tibet. He combined the depth exploration of Jung and the Buddhist discipline that Lamas practiced in the painting of their religious mandalas.

When she began painting the mandalas at home, Madeleine started to attract students who wanted to learn Wise's approach. In addition to the Buddhist discipline of one hundred percent attention at the tip of the brush, and letting the subject emerge rather than imposing a form on the paper, Madeleine introduced a journaling practice, evoking the personal significance of the images that emerged. She valued quiet so that she could do her work in contemplation.

When I came home to become her caregiver, a major adjustment was required by both of us. I did not realize the extent to which I carried the union and the political environment of the province within my psyche. In my mind, I was constantly scanning the horizon for threats or telltale signs of trouble. My job required acute awareness of potential and emerging problems. I was alert for potential problems. When I used that mental orientation in the work of caring for Madeleine, I saw nothing but problems. Her failing health and limited ability to care for herself foreshadowed the prospect of her death from the disease.

We went through a few weeks of adjustment struggle. Then one day she said to me, "If you cannot be with me, it would be better if you were not trying to care for me." After we talked through the significance of what she meant, I realized that my mind was not at ease, and my energy was constantly projecting into the future. In the future, there was nothing but pain and loss. The emotional disturbance was affecting how I was in the present. In fact, I was hardly in the present moment at all.

I had to learn a new way of being. I needed to practice awareness of the present without letting my imagination jump forward into the future. I did not foresee what a demanding exercise "presencing" would be. The word I used described actively being in the present moment. If I was preparing her lunch, my full attention had to be on that task. I needed to catch my mind as it wandered to what came after this moment. Little by little, it got easier. With practice, I became more adjusted to living in the now, and giving it my full attention.

As I adjusted my inner focus to the present, Madeleine let me know that she was aware of the change in me, and found me much easier to be around. I started to be in the present most of the time and I connected to everyone and everything more fully Eventually, I started to find it hard to think about the future and instead of letting my thoughts create a fearful future I was able to completely focus on what I was doing and the person I was present with.

During the remission period after I became her caregiver, Madeleine resumed painting in her studio, welcomed her students to paint with her, and shared her spiritual view of the work. She would instruct each one, and noted the progress that they were making. With some, she just conversed, believing they were not any longer in need of teaching.

After only a year or so, she could no longer climb the stairs to her studio, and she stopped painting. I know that it bothered her not to paint. I watched her strength diminish and realized that her journey to the end of life was continuing.

The community care nursing team offered practical help. They accessed the Red Cross, who provided her aids to make sitting more comfortable. They offered to bring in a hospital bed but she did not want that change. Mornings she would ask me to assist her to descend the stairs from our second floor bedroom. The community care nurses offered to come in to see her several times a week, but after a few times, she asked them not to come, saying that I would provide for her needs.

During this time, a couple were conducting light therapy for Madeleine. On one occasion when they came to the house, they asked if they could dowse the house for energy.

In their scan of the house, one of them used a long flexible wire wand with a weight at the end, and the other used two L-shaped rods made of copper. Working separately, they walked through the house checking it with their instruments. When they reconvened, they described that their instruments reacted to a stimulus in exactly the same places in the house. They interpreted the reaction as geopathic energy emanating from the ground deep beneath the house. Their research suggested that they had uncovered "geopathic stress zones,[7]" electromagnetic radiations that rise up through fault lines. They are considered very harmful to human health. People who have worked with this energy have discovered that there is a strong correlation between cancer and geopathic energy zones.

My interest was raised and I found an epidemiological study in Germany that strongly suggested concentration between cancers and the presence of geopathic fault lines.

---

[7] For further information about geopathic stress see:
http://geopathicstress.us/home

I made L- shaped copper rods from coat hangers and walked through my house by myself. I was surprised that my rods responded in the same place as the ones held by the investigator. Alarmingly, the energy showed up running through the side of the king size bed that Madeleine slept on, but not on my side. Downstairs in the living room, the rods reacted to the geopathic energy running through where her chair was placed for viewing the television.

Conversation with other dowsers indicated there was a general familiarity with the phenomenon. I set about looking for ways to mitigate the effect of the geopathic energy. My healing friends recommended several ways they had heard about, and one of them has worked completely.

I found that I had a facility with the L rods. I read about dowsing, and practiced locating things with the rods. Through repeated practice, I have developed a facility, achieving surprising results. While dowsing is most commonly associated with finding underground water, it is also regularly used to find buried pipes and oil tanks. I have used my rods successfully to find lost jewelry and other items.

Madeleine had resumed teaching mandala work and was seeing a smaller number of students. One evening, before retiring, she asked me if I thought the rods could detect a negative energy disturbance for her. I told her that I could only ask the rods if I could use them that way. She thought that perhaps someone's disturbed energy had stayed with her after a session. To my amazement, the rods responded in the affirmative. In my practice with the rods, when they swung out they were indicating a 'yes' and when they moved into a crossing position, they indicated the answer was no. I could only ask questions that could be answered with a yes or no.

When I asked if Madeleine had attracted negative energy, the rods move into the open V position, indicating that the answer was yes. I asked if I could clear the energy, and again the answer was positive. Then my question was 'how', but I could not ask a question that the rods could not answer in a yes or no. I explored some options for moving the energy, and I got a strong positive from the rods when I asked if the energy would clear with a Reiki blessing. When I used the blessing I had learned from my Reiki teacher, the rods indicated that the negative energy had gone.

By this time, I had done considerable reading in the new cosmology. What I learned is that energy – all the energy that will ever be in the universe – flared out all at once. That energy is the source of all matter. What appears to our senses to be solid is in reality made up of fields of energy in the form of subatomic particles – atoms and molecules. We are made of the same energy that created the universe. We are at the crest of a continuing evolutionary event. Moreover, we are surrounded by electromagnetic energy. Cell phones, radio and television, microwaves and electric stoves, the wires that carry electricity through the buildings we live and work in are all carrying electromagnetism into our everyday lives. I should not have been surprised that simple copper rods would be sensitive to the impulses of energy. What amazed me at that time was that the energy was responding to specific questions. It seems that we are located in a sea of consciousness.

In a practical way, I am connecting to what the scientists have been telling us about the universe. My rodding experience has been a union of the scientific and spiritual. I am in touch with conscious energy that responds to my questions. I am using my mind to look for information.

However it happens, I am drawing from the field, which scientists describe as the state that holds the universe's experience. The zero point field is like a quantum memory that records the entire experience of creation from the beginning. Every human thought or word becomes part of the field, and goes into the shaping of the unfolding thrust of the universe.

I am convinced that the more we understand the nature of the universe, especially the new cosmology, the more we can see more deeply into our spiritual yearnings. As authors such as Thomas Berry express the deep connection between the new story and the deepest aspirations of human mind, there is a healing of the breach. Seekers into the mystery are able give voice to their quest. The upsurge of insight into the universe is fuelling an expanding understanding of cosmology, and I am learning from it as metaphor for the truth at the heart of the cosmos.

My exploration of the scientific findings about the universe is not focused on the mechanics of physics and astronomy. Rather I see the breakthroughs in understanding offering the human more comprehensive knowledge about who and where we are in the story of the unfolding. We are the generation of humans who have the potential of reuniting science and spirit into a unified way of knowing. As I explore the exponential growth in knowledge about the universe, I see more clearly the foundation of spiritual teaching. The primordial teacher about our place in nature is the cosmos.

Seeing how energy is continually creating and unifying, moving ahead and destroying, we see the pulsating property of the substance of the universe. There is no new life that does not expire. I can examine that through the scientific metaphor or I can see the spiritual one. Both take me deeper into the mystery of the single truth.

Madeleine and I knew that we were on the journey to the end of life. For her, the end was anticipated. Her spiritual work with the mandala had prepared her. I was the one who struggled to accept the end of her life's journey. I was committed to accompany her, however long or short it would be. It turned out to be five years longer than either of us thought.

She often told me of a recurring dream/vision. She saw herself walking down a dark corridor, but at the end, there was an open door and bright light shined out. As she looked at the doorway, she saw her deceased mother standing in a welcoming pose.

Madeleine knew that she would be going through the door, and that love awaited her.

As her mind prepared for death, her body rallied and did not decline at the pace she would have liked. Months passed. The door vision dimmed, and Madeleine was saddened that she did not go through when she was ready. Our doctor, who saw her regularly at home, told her that her body was surprisingly strong and had a mind of its own.

In the days we had together, we resolved to communicate fully. There was no reason to leave anything unsaid, or leave regrets that we wished we had told each other something important. The conversations were very kind. We each held the other with tenderness and compassion. I often think of those days as though we were in a dream. There had been a lot of fighting in our earlier years, but the last period of our union was warm and gentle.

I had always thought of us as two trees in an orchard. We each had our sturdy trunk, rooted deeply in the earth. Our branches intertwined, but we remained independent in our side-by-side connection. During the years of our journey to her death, there was a change. As Madeleine grew more dependent on my care, I found myself bursting with compassion. My heart cracked open, and I learned to love in a new way. I learned to give without expecting anything in return. There was no keeping mental accounts as before. I simply met her in the moment, and did what was needed. I found a new generosity, and a new willingness to be present to her. A quote from William Shakespeare comes to mind.

> *"The more I give to thee, the more*
> *I have, for both are infinite.[8]"*

My heart ached, both to see her deteriorate and to know that she would be passing through the membrane that separated the living from the dead. She asked me to use the rods to ask about her sense of having visitors from the spirit world. I was in for another surprise. In the years of being without religion, I was prepared to accept that when you die your energy returns to the stream. Now I was being asked to use the rods to investigate the presence of particular individuals that had died, possibly years ago in some cases. What I found was a consistent and varied presence of people connected by bonds of family, love and a lasting commitment to one another.

---

[8] William Shakespeare, *Romeo and Juliet*, Act 2, Scene 2

Whenever I asked, the rods reported that Madeleine's mother was always with her. On the other hand, when she asked about her father, he was rarely there. Other family members came and went. Her sister Mary was present most often. Her younger brother Louis would visit often. Other members of her family or deceased friends would come as well. She would wonder aloud whether any of the spirits that surrounded her had messages for her. Mostly the answer was that they were there to support her and to keep her company. She never asked about their world, and was content with whatever answer came through the rods.

When the end came, it came quickly. Strength left her body one night as we were going up the stairs together. I called our doctor, and he had the palliative care team from the Victoria Hospice make an emergency call to the house. With impressive efficiency and care, they made Madeleine comfortable and began to give her sedatives for her pain. Our doctor came a few hours later and gave the nurses directions for the drug levels, and by the early morning Madeleine was dead.

I discovered her at 3 am. The emergency nurse from Hospice pronounced her dead, and removed the kit they had brought to see to her needs. Alone with my wife of thirty-six years, I was overcome. Kneeling by her body, I cried until the sun came up. In first light, when I saw her face, I was overwhelmed by the peace that had come back into her expression. Her beauty in death was radiant. All the suffering that had been etched on her face from years of contending with the disease were erased. She was translucent.

As I looked at her in the light of dawn, I recalled what I had heard in a workshop about death and grieving. The former chaplain said that ancient cultures believed that the spirit stayed with the body for a period after physical death. Entertaining that thought, I picked up the dowsing rods and asked if I could be in contact with Madeleine's spirit. The rods swung into the affirmative position. I asked if she was with her mother and her sister. The rods indicated a no. I was surprised. Asking a different way, I inquired if she was now with her guardian spirit. Again, no. I then asked if she was still here in the room with me. This time the rods swung vigorously to the yes position.

I was engulfed by sacredness. I got a basin of warm water and washed her. Knowing there was more I could do to extend the sacred moment, I began to anoint her. Starting with her face and head, I slowly applied the oil to every area of her body.

When I had completed the ritual, I was depleted. I went downstairs and made a pot of tea. When I came back to the bedroom with my tea, I sensed that there was a different energy in the room. I had a sense her spirit was not there.

With the rods close by, I asked if I could be in contact with Madeleine. The rods swung to the yes position. I asked if I was communicating with Madeleine, I needed a sign. The rod in my left hand swung completely around and pointed to my heart. I asked her if she was still in the room with her body, and the answer was no. I asked her if she was at peace. Yes. Was she with her guardian spirit? Yes. Was she with her mother and her sister and brother? Yes. I asked her a question that I don't know where it came from. I asked, "Are you in time?" The rods said no. "Are you in some place?" Again, no. "Are you conscious?" Yes. "Will you always be able to communicate with me?" Yes. "And will I be able to communicate with you?" Yes.

I have been able to make contact with Madeleine's energy in the years since that extraordinary moment. What is beyond doubt for me is that Madeleine's spirit is in the universe and is able to interact with me.

I communicate with the energy body of the person I knew and loved on Earth. There is two-way communication. The once incarnated energy abides intact. I have had to change my mind about personal survival beyond the membrane we call death.

In addition to the peace I feel at having a continuing connection to all my deceased loved ones, this experience confirmed the substance of my new understanding of the universe. On a very personal level, the new cosmology was affirmed for me. The basis of spirituality is in the universe, and it is critically important to understand.

8

MY RETURN TO LIFE

Today, something is happening to the whole structure of human consciousness. A fresh kind of life is starting. Driven by the forces of love, the fragments of the world are seeking each other, so that the world may come into being.

PIERRE TEILHARD DE CHARDIN

Madeleine was gone. After five years of intense care giving, I was alone, surrounded by absence. The house was empty. I was alone with my memories and grief. The pain was intense; I could not assimilate it for quite a while.

For most of my working life, my world had been defined by service. Cancer had reshaped Madeleine's independence, and mine. We became interdependent in a new way; each looking to the other. Although, at the beginning of my care giving I would not have bet on my ability to stay committed to a long term role as attendant, my choice came down to a decision each day. I chose to meet her needs, cook and serve appetizing meals, and attend to the reality of daily living. The circumference of my attention had grown small indeed. As she progressively neared the threshold between life and death, I neared that portal with her. Even though I knew that she was walking that path alone, I was traveling in lock step with her. By fully attending to her in each moment, I moved into sync with her. When she died, being alive seemed strange. Not only was my partner gone, my purpose was ripped away once again, and I felt intensely alone.

I had the feeling of falling into an abyss. I had had a similar feeling after leaving the priesthood, but this was more intense. During the years of my accompanying Madeleine to the end of her life, my heart had cracked open and I had learned to love in a new way: more completely, less self-interested, purer in spirit. The loss was more intense than any other feeling I had ever known.

There were practical things to do. I placed an obituary in the paper, notified key people and asked them to tell others that Madeleine was dead. I arranged for the Memorial Society to have her body cremated, and I planned a memorial for her three weeks after her death. I decided to preside at the memorial, chose music, and asked people to speak about her. The service was held in the auditorium of the John T. Shields building, the union's building in Victoria that they had named in my honour. The room was filled to capacity and beyond as our friends, including our dearest friends from Texas, her mandala students, people from the community and her family from Toronto gathered. I also invited family and close friends to a dinner to continue to talk about her and celebrate her life.

In the immediate aftermath of her death, I could not engage in anything. I could not even go to the spirituality circle I facilitated, much less take on my role at Leadership Victoria. I was anchored in the vortex of a black hole.

When, after months of intense grieving, I was ready for some kind of activity, I set about turning my house into a museum of Madeleine's art. Seventeen large mandalas comprised the legacy of her work as an artist. Each piece took about a year to paint and was a symbolic map of her life and a picture of her innermost being. I framed all the paintings, and hung them in the house until every available wall space held one of her mandalas.

Years before, the Tibetan Buddhist monks had come to Victoria to construct a mandala from grains of coloured sand. Painstakingly, the monks added one grain of sand at a time for weeks until the mandala was complete. The Dalai Lama had visited the Victoria Art Gallery during the making of the mandala and at a public reception thanked Madeleine for using her mandalas to publicize the event.

At the end of the monk's visit, when the exquisitely beautiful mandala was completed, the monks swept up the sand and poured it into the sea. The act was a demonstration of non-attachment. That was a reminder of the impermanence of all things, which is one of the tenets at the heart of Buddhist teaching. Not only did they make no effort to preserve the unique work of art, they consciously destroyed it. The occasion greatly influenced Madeleine and she wanted to follow in that tradition. She had asked that I give away many of her mandalas and I put my energy into distributing the paintings according to her wishes.

In the months that followed, I realized how easy it would have been for me to continue to live in the anteroom to death. I continued to focus on Madeleine, her wishes and her estate. When spring arrived with new life, the cherry blossoms and the daffodils, I noticed that the universe had moved on and renewed itself. As I walked in nature, in the beautiful gardens in Victoria, I realized I had a choice. I could ignore the impulse of the cycle of the seasons and stay focused on death, or I could choose to come back to life with the rest of nature. Then I noticed that I did not know how to do that.

My habit of staying in the present moment had taken over from my previous orientation to the future. I did not want to go back the way I had been as head of the union, calculating my life to meet future goals. How could I rejoin the world without calculating the steps it in my head? I sat in my garden and meditated on that question.

The answer that came to me was profound. I could say, "Yes" to the universe. I had developed the conviction that I am in this world to contribute to the unfolding of the universe. I intuited that I am part of an intricate cosmic pattern that is tending toward life. I resolved to affirm whatever the universe presented me.

The first thing to happen after this decision was a call from Leadership Victoria. I was the Chair of the Board, responsible for the delivery of community-based training for volunteer leadership in the region. The Programme Director had informed the Executive that she had to take a leave for health reasons and asked me if I would take over her role. The Leadership class met as a group once a month for a community learning day, and each meeting had a committee responsible for organizing and conducting the event. There were also group projects that teams of the participants were planning and carrying out. The Leadership Victoria office oversaw both these events, and someone had to hold the reins until she returned, which she estimated to be about six weeks. I said, yes, I would step in and ensure that the programme continued.

Six weeks turned into six months. I went to work downtown every day, and coordinated Leadership Victoria for the term of the medical leave. I had not administered an organization since I stepped down from the BCGEU presidency six years before and I was suddenly busy and challenged.

Sally, a woman I had known since my days at Victoria Family and Children's Services, called and suggested that I recruit a friend of hers to become a volunteer on the Curriculum Committee. She gave me a description of the skills and background of the woman she had in mind. She had a PhD in curriculum development and had done international development and peace work in Latin America. She was currently doing contract work focused on indigenous education. She sounded perfect for Leadership Victoria. Moreover, she was doing some contract work for a NGO whose office was in the same building where my office was located. I resolved to get in touch.

After a few abortive attempts to meet up, I dropped into her office and invited the prospective volunteer to lunch. We fell into comfortable conversation right away. Even before we ordered lunch, we were in a deep and engaging conversation. On so many levels, I connected warmly with Robin. Our lunch extended over two hours. She was beautiful, intelligent, and charming. She had spent much of her life working for peace and social justice, as had I. By the end of our lunch, my interest had shifted from organizational to personal and I wanted to get to know this woman better.

The chance came the next week. Sally was organizing a fundraiser for another local charity. She was selling tickets. I agreed to buy one, and she mentioned that Robin had also bought a ticket to the event. I immediately called Robin and invited her to go with me to Sal's event. She readily agreed.

I found myself in an awkward position. I had not
dated anyone since I was a teenager. Madeleine
and I had not dated. We began as working
partners. Close creative engagement in the context
of our mutual work for the church drew us
together, but we repressed any open expression of
physical attraction for the four years we worked
together for the church. The friendship turned to
love, but sexuality was not the foundation of our
love. In any new partner, I wanted a balance of
love, mutual interests, emotional compatibility, and
a healthy sex life.

As part of the resolution to our marriage dilemma,
Madeleine had given me her blessing to have
sexual relations with other women. Our marriage
had been based on mutual respect and a love from
the beginning but did not include much physical
intimacy. Through the thirty-six years of our
marriage, I had been sexually attracted to other
women. I was not promiscuous nor was I inclined
to take advantage of all the sexual opportunities
that came my way.

I also realized I was a complicated individual who
had started my life as a priest, committed to
celibacy. I needed to work through the hang-ups
that came with more than a decade of trying to

avoid gossip and public scandal. I had always feared scandal. My wish to protect my reputation as well as my sense of decency was always in play.

For the fourteen years I was union president, I had lived alone during the week in an apartment near my office. I had a love affair with woman who was sensitive to my circumstance. I was in a high profile position and aware of the attendant risk of negative publicity that would have resulted from any scandal. She was discrete and protective of my reputation.

My lover cared deeply for me and had loved me for many years. She wanted a normal relationship, but I was not free and did not want to lead her on. While I was in a sexless marriage, it was a marriage I was committed to, and I constrained myself from publicly dating anyone. I never felt free.

At the stage my grieving was in when I first met Robin, I was not looking for a new relationship. Because I had given expression to all the intense feelings as they arose, that energy was spent, but I was still periodically gripped by loss. Deep heartrending anguish would wash over me unbidden and unexpected. Although I was near the end of the intense grief, the loss of Madeleine still affected me. I was unsure if I could enter a relationship. I was venturing into unknown territory.

The Victoria Hospice program had a counselling service for people affected by the death of a loved one. I had been seeing a therapist since Madeleine's death, and he was aware of the state of my heart. I sought his wisdom as a sounding board. I wondered whether falling in love during the grieving process would nullify the love or diminish the grief. What he advised me was that I was not betraying the departed loved one by experiencing the joy of new love. I would always remember her. I confided in him that I had contacted her with the rods to ask if I was offending her by opening my heart to someone new. The answer through the rods was no, and that she blessed me the joy of finding someone to love fully. The therapist said that life will always seek a way to embrace love. He thought I was one of the most fortunate of men to find true love at any time in life.

Fortunate! I was indeed privileged to find someone who loves me wholly and fully. I often remind myself that Robin came into my orbit when I said yes to the universe, and we continue to be conscious of the gift in both our lives.

I am older than Robin by fifteen years. The difference in age was a question for Robin, but it turned out not to be an obstacle. I understood that I would continue to grow older, but that does not mean that I would become aged in the process. In my experience, our relationship has invigorated me, kept my interests current, and prompted me to find ways to continue the contribution I enjoy making to the world. Being receptive to her energy and interests, I am renewed, and my response-ability increases.

In addition to the sweetness of my relationship with Robin, I received another delightful surprise. I was given the opportunity to experience fatherhood. Robin's daughter Nicola was nineteen and attending university at McGill in Montreal at the beginning of our relationship. She came home at the end of the semester, and was highly curious about the man who was in love with her mom. Robin had warned me that in the past Nikki had been hostile to men who were courting her. Nikki thought them unworthy of her. By the end of the summer, Nikki had captured my heart with her generosity and openness. She continues to grow into an unusually intelligent and vibrant young woman, with interests that take her deeply into the ecological movement and link her passion for aboriginal justice. To my delight, she was open to a relationship with me that allows us to relate as father and daughter.

Nikki has not seen her father in many years. Robin raised Nikki on her own, without the father's involvement. Since I have never had children, I am happy that she welcomes me as a paternal influence in her life. I feel singularly blessed to be met in my love for her, and that she includes me in her life as her father. Her love is one of the most delicious gifts of a generous universe.

I have found that by saying 'yes' to the stream of events that the universe has sent my way, my life has overflowed with abundance. I have taken jobs that have been interesting and rewarding. Since Robin and I have been married, we moved to a breathtaking home on a Gulf Island while I served as Executive Director at an educational centre and then began teaching at Vancouver Island University. When I took up a fellowship at the Centre for the Study of Religion and Society at the University of Victoria we moved back to Victoria and I continue to teach at VIU and volunteer as the head of the Centre for Earth and Spirit.

Observing the opportunities that have flown from these responses, my life has been enriched with new friends, with a flow of income that keeps us well, and an expanding opportunity to deepen and expand. I could not have designed the path as well as the one that opened in response to my responding to the opening doors, and the closing ones. Sometimes the greatest insight and benefits came from the things I stumbled over and from the pain that ensued. Those missteps created learning and benefits as much as the things that went well.

My journey from religion to spirituality was not a straight line. Nonetheless, there were some clear steps along the way. I began with a commission from my grandfather that I would play a role of religious leader: "the first American Pope." My family was religious, and I was raised with a strong sense of a divine presence. I went from home to the seminary to train to become a priest. I grew close to the sacred, participating in the symbolic sacramental rituals of the ancient church.

In the seminary, I learned modern science, which had uncovered new information about the Bible, the foundation stone of Judaism and Christianity. The new revelation severely undermined many of the suppositions that formed the basis of

Christian belief. The universe was providing an opportunity to renew and reform many of the outmoded expressions of religion. Spirit had given religion an excellent opportunity "to say yes." A strong new consciousness was impelling the church to acknowledge contemporary revelation. When the church broke faith with that call, I lost faith in the church.

I had to step blindly into the secular when I left the church, reentering the world, with all the demands to survive in modern life. One of the requirements of this reentry was sexuality, which I did not handle very well. I did better with work. Social work, counselling and supervising new workers came easily. In responding to that environment, I said yes to union work. I learned to be a warrior defending the rights of others and rose to the demands of leadership. I learned the art of politics and stood up on behalf of public services. In pursuing the hero's journey, I was given the gift of a vision. I came to understand the mythic and how it was operating in me. One of the biggest steps on my way to spirituality was the recognition that the inner world creates the outer and that there is energy in the synchronization of the two.

Discovery of the mythic in my psyche opened the door to the wonders of the universe. This inflow of transformative insight was the most impacting discovery on my journey. The profound change that has emerged from very recent breakthroughs is providing humanity with an entirely new set of concepts that reunites consciousness, spirit and matter. My thinking was reoriented. I discovered spirit in the universe.

Part of the effect of the cosmological discovery led me back to Earth. In nature, I came into harmony with the flow of creative energy. The environment is the universe made immediate. We come from it, and we are relearning to hold it sacred. Along with a re-appreciation of the wild, I have developed a new respect for the First Nations of the world.

My spirituality journey took another dimension when I learned to be a caregiver for Madeleine on her journey to the end of her life. The opportunity to deepen in my sense of living in the present moment was a gift of being with someone who knew they were dying and needed to live intensively in the present. The benefits of living in love and service without strings flowed to me during those six years.

During much of the time I was a caregiver, I facilitated a group for men seeking to develop spirituality in their lives. On a weekly basis, the group came together and shared at a profound level of trust and openness. In the energy of the circle, I came into direct contact with spiritual energy.

At heart, the understanding that I am an integral element of the conscious, living universe has reshaped my orientation to the universal realm. An unbroken chain of being connects me to the beginning. The unity of the cosmos connects me to all. The unfolding nature of time and space puts me at the leading edge of cosmic evolution. There is purpose in everything I do and say. I am part of the blossoming of consciousness. I am a part of the All.

9

DANCING ON THE CUTTING EDGE

You must live in the present, launch yourself on
every wave, find your eternity in each moment.

HENRY DAVID THOREAU

The Cosmos as context

The internal dynamic of the unfolding universe is
so unified that everything that it manifests is part
of the oneness. We are just becoming aware that
consciousness and spirit are its characteristics from
the very first energy impulse. The universe that is
generating itself embraces everything in its unity.

Swimme and Berry assert that from the moment of
the great flaring forth, the universe develops in
such a way that each event is woven into the fabric
of every other. They say that protons may be
thought of as being in a place, but also just as
legitimately present to all the particles that they
have ever interacted with. Unity of time and place
puts everything into a single web of connection.
"No part of the present can be isolated from any

207

other part of the present or the past or the future."[9] This was a strange and wonderful notion. I was excited to think that I might have found the key I was looking for.

My excitement rose as I began to digest what the quantum physicist, David Bohm, added to this proposition. He concluded that all matter in the universe is interconnected by quantum waves. He referred to ... "an overwhelming sense of 'unbroken wholeness' in the world."[10] In a universe of unbroken wholeness, death would be an earthly experience, but not necessarily a change within the universe.

Because there is a continuity of everything in the universe, the evolutionary process has produced a seamless unfolding from the beginning of the emergence of time. The energy that has generated that blossoming of the cosmos is conscious and spirit filled. Each person that has evolved from the primordial dynamic is connected and stays connected to the continuous creative flow.

---

[9] Brian Swimme and Thomas Berry, *The Universe Story, From the Primordial Flaring Forth to the Ecozoic Era – A Celebration of the Unfolding of the Cosmos,* San Francisco, Harper Collins, 1992, p. 29 p. 29

[10] Cited by Lynne McTaggart, *The Field: Quest for the Secret Force of the Universe,* (New York, NY: HarperCollins, 2002)

Another force in the evolution of the universe is attraction. Brian Swimme calls this force "allurement." Gravity is a manifestation of the universe's power of attraction. From the smallest protons to the swirling galaxies, attraction creates the shape of the cosmos. In the context of human presence on earth, allurement can be seen as love.

In a conscious universe, love is a binding, uniting force. I feel it in nature when I watch the eagle soar and am mesmerized by a passing whale. I know that the love that is stirred in me is an attracting force. Love of the animals in my life is something I experience at a different level. These creatures that so openly give love and devotion activate a deep bond.

Love has long been the song of poets and artists. I have been blessed by an abundance of love in my life. My parents and grandparents, extended family, and the circle of friends whom I love have taught me to open my heart. The women who have connected to me with tenderness and intimacy have invited me to venture more deeply into love, and evoked change throughout my life. Pain and sorrow combine with deep passion and openheartedness to generate a well of the experience of love to transform.

As I call to mind the people in my life whom I have loved and who are now dead, the bond of love is still strong and active. Death has not diminished my feeling of tenderness and connection. I think of them and experience their presence. Consciousness crosses the divide between this life and the ongoing flow of time.

Because I am interested in how individuals, as points of energy individuated in time, persist in the universe beyond death, I looked first at traditional wisdom. Every tradition and every culture has had some sense of an abiding presence of human spirit. Each tradition has a way of speaking about the intuition of ongoing individual consciousness that is similar, and at the same time, unique.

The sense of continuity beyond death is ancient. Chi, or qi, spirit, soul, prana, and kundalini were all ways that the world's religious traditions and many First Nations mythologies have spoken about the life force. All continued beyond death. Each tradition drew on the way they understood the universe to put language to their intuition about an afterlife.

All the diverse ways of thinking in the past and the new insights are united within the concept of cosmic energy. The universe is a single unified actor, conscious and alive. The universe is spiritual and loving. Everything that is comes out of the single integrated whole. The insight that the universe is a coherent whole, containing and preserving everything within itself was consistent with my rodding experience.

Bruce Lipton discovered that there is awareness at the cellular level. Deep emotions such as fear or love will send a cascade of chemicals to the cells, and the entire organism responds with a high level of communication triggering different responses depending on the environment in the cell.[11]

Berry has no difficulty saying that the universe is sentient. Berry observes that "in the late twentieth century...empirical inquiry into the universe reveals that from its beginning in the galactic system to its earthly expression in human consciousness, the universe carries within itself a psychic-spiritual as well as a physical-material dimension. Otherwise, human consciousness emerges out of nowhere... In reality the human activates the most profound dimension of the

---

[11] Bruce Lipton, *The Biology of Belief: Unleashing the Power of Consciousness, Matter and Miracles*, (New York, Hay House Inc. 20050

universe itself, its capacity to reflect on and celebrate itself in conscious self-awareness."[12]

Consciousness is not terminated at death. My experience of being able to communicate with loved ones who have gone through the membrane that encloses this life, convinces me that the state of awareness is not dependent on physical form. The energy that is at once past, present and future carries consciousness and spirit, and bridges the condition of this life and the state we call death.

Discerning the cutting edge

The metaphor for my place in the universe is a surfer riding in the curl of a perfect wave. I am the surfer who becomes one with the energy, rides the breaking edge, and I surf along the leading edge with serenity.

This metaphor is inspired by the knowledge of the universe story I have acquired in the last twenty years. Since NASA captured the graphic images of the Cosmic Background Radiation with its COBE probe in the early 90s, the scientific community has

---

[12] Thomas Berry, *Dream of the Earth* (San Francisco, Sierra Club Books, 1990), pp. 131-132

come to near unanimity in developing a picture of the beginning of the cosmos.

In the beginning, originating power brought forth the universe from a state of pure potential. The incipient universe burst forth in an intense flaring of heat, light and power. As Swimme and Berry describe it, "All the energy that would ever exist in the entire course of time erupted as a single quantum – a singular gift – existence. If in the future, stars would blaze and lizards would blink in their light, these actions would be powered by the same numinous energy that flared forth at the dawn of time."[13]

I find it impossible to adequately visualize that quantum of energy either at the beginning or now, almost fourteen billion years later. I imagine at the beginning that when the universe erupted into being, a small intense incredibly hot ball of conscious energy, seething with power, a soup of swirling particles and atoms. Because time/space expands as a single dimension, when the universe was only moments old (time), the space that the energy quantum existed within was relatively tiny.

---

[13] Swimme and Berry, p17

At the beginning, from the field of pure possibility, particles emerged from the density of compacted energy. With unimaginably great heat, light flowed forth into the void, creating time and space as it expanded. The beginning is not an event in time. The origin did not take place in time or space. Time and space begin with the flaring forth. The universe is a coherent whole of which time and space are essential constituents.

Now, 13.7 billion years after the initial flaring, we find ourselves on Earth, orbiting a star in a side arm of the Milky Way galaxy, one of hundreds of billions of galaxies that have emerged within the universe. Within the past twenty years we have discovered a massive amount about the beginning and the nature of our universe. What do we know about the present?

Einstein concluded that time and space, which we experience as two dimensions, are aspects of a single phenomenon. In the scientific world, they refer to this as time/space. Contemporary cosmologists conclude that the characteristics of time/space were determined by the universe in the tiniest fraction of a second after the great flaring. The strength of the gravitational force and the electromagnetic field, as well as the two nuclear interactions would govern the nature of the cosmic activity within the overriding unity. These relationships, adopted by the universe right at the beginning, would determine how fast the universe would expand and the nature of all its subsequent relationships. The height of the tallest mountain, the shape of fish and animals and flowers and the size of humans are determined by the ratios that the universe adopted at the beginning. Had there been the tiniest variation in either direction, the universe could not have developed at all.

In the energy of the initial flaring, the searing heat creates the first elements, which in turn combine and cause the energy field to expand. The symmetry of the fundamental architecture of the cosmos begins to shape future. The density fluctuations of the earliest stages will be imprinted on the unfolding, giving eventual shape to the formation of galaxies. As the expansion cools, the wild creation and annihilation of elements that characterized the earliest stages ceased and the coherence took on an elegant form.

Cosmologists have looked at the expansion of the energy and observed that over time, the energy cooled and the outward thrust of the energy generated quantum fluctuations or ripples. The gas clouds containing the primal elements were ignited, flaring into galaxies and stars.

In the process of the outward direction of the early universe, the expansion of gases and the electromagnetic energy field set not just one galaxy into existence but hundreds of billions. Some scientists calculate that there could easily be 500 billion. Each of these galaxies could contain hundreds of billions of stars, too many to actually count.

The ability to speak about the age of the universe comes from the calculation of the time it would take light traveling at 300,000 kilometers per second to reach Earth. Based on those calculations, astrophysicists have narrowed the age of the universe down to approximately 13.7 billion years.

The Hubble telescope began peering back into the origin of the earliest galactic formation. Using the speed of light as a measure, Hubble scientists were able to determine the age of the universe. The universe is not five thousand years old as was assumed a mere hundred years ago. According to a recent story in the Christian Science Monitor, the refurbished Hubble satellite has captured images from when the universe was only between six hundred million to eight hundred million years old.[14]

NASA is also is responsible for another less well known spacecraft that is measuring changes in heat within the universe since the time of the Big Bang. Following the COBE measurement of the cosmic background radiation, NASA launched the Wilkinson Microwave Anisotropy Probe (WMAP) in 2001. The intent was to measure the radiant heat of the expanding cosmic radiation across the full sky. WMAP is responsible for graphically depicting the expansion of the universe in space and time from the beginning to now.[15]

The highest precision instrument ever devoted to the exploration of the universe has produced a map-like diagram of history and shape of the cosmos. The image shows the expansion of space/time, and shows how the universe has developed. Over the course of thirteen point seven billion years, the expanse of space correlates to the duration of time.

---

[14] Peter N. Spotts. "Hubble telescope glimpses universe's earliest galaxies." The Christian Science Monitor, Jan 5, 2010. *http://www.csmonitor.com/USA/2010/0105/Hubble-telescope-glimpses-universe-s-earliest-galaxies*

[15] National Aeronautics and Space Administration, Wilkinson Microwave Anisotropy Probe. *http://map.gsfc.nasa.gov/*

The shape of the cosmos surprised me. The expanse is not circular as the ancients thought. WMAP shows the development of the universe has expanded in linear shape. But neither is it infinite. The thrust of the early expansion, called the inflation phase, pushed time/space outward, largely determining the subsequent linear shape of time/space. Over the ensuing millennia, the expanse of the universe has matched its extension in time. The universe developed in an evolutionary process. The probe shows that the development of the cosmos along the time axis is comparable to its growth in space.

As Einstein predicted, time and space flow in a linear direction. The WMAP shows that the universe experienced its greatest growth at the very beginning of time. There is no evidence that anywhere in the universe there is either time beyond now or space beyond where we are. Infatuation with the future, or with time travel into the future seems to be only possible in the imagination. Likewise, the ancient image of a cyclical universe in which time rotates with the heavens, an eternal past, is not supported by the discoveries of WMAP. The belief in the mandala of time, where history is continually repeated, has been supplanted by the discoveries of modern science.

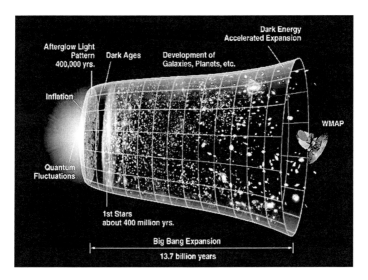

Figure 2: WMAP History of Universe

Cosmologists point out that the universe is an ongoing energy event, and the image confirms the unity of the expansion. The entire history of the universe is not lost. It becomes present in this moment. The continuing unfolding of the cosmos, taking place in time, produces the now.

The expansion from the nucleus of the Big Bang expands in direct proportion to the duration. The space of the universe is finite, and can be grasped as a multivalent "here". Importantly, WMAP demonstrates that there is no future beyond the present moment. The frame in which the data was collected by WMAP contains the past and present, but nothing beyond the now. This highly sophisticated analysis of the microwave heat in the universe proves that there is no time beyond now and no space outside the universe. Everything, therefore, is happening now, at the edge of the expanding cosmos. We are on the cutting edge of space and time.

I am excited by the idea that we are in the moment at which the entire universe is unfolding. The universe has created this moment and this place. It has been developing for almost fourteen billion years to bring this moment into being. The entire evolutionary history of the Earth has been for this moment. Everything that the universe has experienced continues into this moment. In the cosmos where no energy is lost and none can be added, we are the focal point of the unfolding. All the energy that has produced the visible universe is present all around us at this moment. What we do with the energy we have determines the nature of the continuing moment.

The way the cosmos has evolved through tumult and chaos, attraction and symmetry, choice and chance, shows the amazing diversity and direction that the universe has chosen. It all comes to fruition in this moment. Everything that has occurred to now has produced this instant. What is in the now is the only thing that can be. As far as we know, there are no alternative universes. Of all the scenarios that might have existed, no other scenarios actually do exist in this moment. Because the universe has created this moment as its culmination, all other possibilities vanish once this moment comes into being. In this moment, we are that which is. We find the groove and align ourselves with the direction that thirteen point seven billion years of evolution has brought about.

The universe has chosen this moment to reveal the knowledge that can make a shift in its unfolding. Each sentient being also manifests in the present, and is aligned to the unfolding. According to quantum theory, there is choice at every level of being. As humans, we have to consciously choose to be in the moment and to accept what is. Our choices are shaping this moment and the next.

Our freedom also allows us not to choose to be present in the moment and to resist what is. By resisting alignment, however, we create stress for ourselves and static in our energy field. On the other hand, when we go with the energy, there is peace and harmony that we experience as flow. We actively contribute to the dynamics that are producing the next moment. When we come into sync with what is, we are like liquid in a deep river. We are not in control of this flow. We are in it and of it, part of the entire cosmos at the leading edge of the time/space.

I have a reverence for all that goes into this moment. The more I get to appreciate the complexity and the simplicity, the more I sense the sacred. The majesty and mystery of how this moment comes about overwhelms my capacity to take things for granted. The sheer creative confluence that brings us into time at this moment is impossible to fully apprehend. There is no doubt in my mind that we are here for a purpose. Since each person, and each sentient being is unique, our contribution to the unfolding of the cosmos is also unique.

Every one of us is an energy centre, reflecting the universe. Like everything else in our cosmos, we are more energy than matter. The energy that animates us is the energy that has given rise to the entire universe. Through the presence of the human in history, the universe has added an evolving consciousness. In the context of our cosmic mission, we are truly participating in the ongoing creation of the emerging universe.

We live at a moment when the mass of evidence gives humanity the ability to surpass the flawed materialistic worldview that shackled the human imagination. If we understand the nature of our participation with the universe as co-creative, we see the divine mystery in our activity. We are of the universe; channeling the energy of the creative fire; emerging in the consciousness of the entire cosmos, revealing the divine. We are matter and spirit in a single form. As such, we allow the divine to show forth another dimension of the sacred in the wonder of this moment.

I am optimistic that the new revelation about and from the universe will produce deep transformation in our social order. Our new thinking about the universe as acting, sentient, self-determining its future is so unlike the older visions that in short order humanity will begin to see the entire world differently.

The new and growing perspective offers the human race a fresh way to understand our collective place on Earth. First, we are coming to appreciate that we descend from the long evolutionary history of the Earth. We are seeing our place in the universe as children of our star, the sun. The sun has given us our energy, climate, food, and the entire context of our lives. Humanity is the product of eons of evolution. At the leading edge of time and the universe's expansion in space, humanity is integral to continuing evolutionary history of the cosmos. I see us in the wave curl of space/time. The universe is not here for us, but rather we are of and for the universe.

Humans now have the capacity to love and feel compassion for others and themselves. People have intelligence and consciousness that enables them to understand what is happening and to assess its significance.

We might act very differently toward the Earth and its creatures if we fully understood that we are of this planet. We are more than visitors on a heavenly journey. We are the stuff of the Earth. A change of perspective about what we are meant to be in the wave curl of time could revolutionize our approach to everything. Rather than viewing the Earth as a basket of goods for our use, we might visualize ourselves as participants in a dynamic community of beings, each with a role and purpose in the diversity of life on Earth. Rather than causing or allowing the destruction of countless numbers of species every day, we might begin respecting and protecting our fellow members of the Earth Community. In addition, we have a collective responsibility for the entire human family. The emerging awareness among humankind is that we need to form a circle of care for one another and the Earth Community of humans and more than humans.

The gift of the universe in our time is the revelation of the singleness and interconnectedness of everything. An abundance of insight is pouring into our awareness that we are creatures of nature. Before it is too late, humanity has the opportunity to reverse out destructive behaviors and begin to preserve the natural world. We know that we have a choice. We can devastate what remains of nature, or we can elect to preserve it or the future of the Earth. We need to take to heart Einstein's wisdom that in order to solve the problems we face we need a different level of thinking than we had when we created them. Where is this new thinking going to come from? I believe that the universe is actively showing us that different level.

In the face of the outpouring of new cosmological workings of the Earth and the universe, I have a growing sense of time speeding up. Perhaps it is an increasing sense of the crisis that the Earth is in, or perhaps it is the universe preparing for another rapid expansion of time/space. With the insight that now is a crucial moment in the unfolding, we have a corresponding responsibility to stay in the curl of energy that is moving us ahead.

The new future at the breaking edge of time has to be about more than stopping the harm and damage. While stopping the degradation of the planet is essential, the universe has more in mind than that. The entire cosmos is poised on the brink of expansion. How it expands depends on the culmination of all that has happened in the past plus what happens in this moment. The range of impulses by all of humanity is constantly impacting the direction of space/time.

In a dance, we feel the rhythm and the tempo of the music. We can discern the flow of the energy in our bodies and we can come into resonance with the harmonics. Dancers feel the energy and respond on an instinctive level. Attunement is something that indicates that we have come into synchronization with the tempo of the events of the moment. I feel that harmony in nature. By the sea, in the mountains or woods, the energy of the surrounding environment brings me into coherence. In cities, surrounded by the humanities imprint, I am often more conscious of the massed talent and ingeniousness of people as they strive to create a humanized environment. At times, however, we are out of coherence with the natural harmonies. I have to refocus my intention to be in harmony with the Earth, meditating, or practicing conscious unity with all being.

Bringing positive emotions into my consciousness shifts my inner presence. I have learned that having a loving attitude is one way to enhance the influence of my human contribution to the universe.

Almost all the creatures in the Earth community instinctively contribute to the wellbeing of the planet simply by being themselves. Nature has attuned each creature to fulfill its highest purpose within the world's interconnected network. Only humans have the highly developed ability to exercise free choice that can lead to our capacity to do things that are not good for the planet and its inhabitants. A higher onus rests on the human to consciously align with the energies of the planet.

The insight about the horizon of time raises the imperative of acting now. The universe does not guarantee a future. Quantum theory points to probability when we attempt to foretell the future. There is a probability that time and space will continue to unfold, as we perceive them to have done in the past, but there is no guarantee. There is only now.

Our discovery about the nature of the expansion of time/space should convince us that we only have this continuing moment to alter our thinking and our behavior. Future generations will have every right to ask us, "What did you do in the time of the world's crisis to save the planet?" If we are to be fully alive to the potential of humanity, we will accelerate our actions to halt the destruction and begin to respect our required contribution to the Earth community.

Have I discovered the spirituality of the universe? I sing with the joy that has come into my heart as I have pursued my search.

BACKWORD

Although, John doesn't include a last chapter of his personal story, I have asked if he might not include it at the end, like an epilogue, but told from an eyewitness account—as it speaks volumes about the interconnectedness of the cosmos.

***

Just before John met his second wife, Robin, my closest friend, she underwent heart surgery. Her heart had been worn out by her long years as an activist/filmmaker for the peace movement in Central America and the environmental movement here in BC. The years of battling for those with no voices, enduring severe conditions, violence and squaring up against the corporate powers had left Robin's heart damaged. It had also been broken by a long and difficult relationship with a revolutionary priest from El Salvador with whom she had a daughter, Nikki. For the first ten years of Nikki's life, they traveled in and out of a war-torn country helping with the movement in of medicine and movement out of films to raise awareness of the causes of the war. Robin tried to convince him to come back to the safety of Canada and raise Nikki there, but he chose to keep his vocation. Robin returned to BC where she sought counseling with an ex-priest on her relationship with Nikki's father, who had an intense vocation for the survival of his people and country, even when the Catholic turned its back on these priests. He had cautioned not to expect her priest to abandon his vows, so she raised her precocious young daughter alone, reengaged in the environmental movement and finished her PhD into Mayan forms of education and world view.

After the heart surgery, Robin announced that it was time to heal her heart and she was going to look for someone that she could love again, be loved back and provide a father to her daughter. She called me up shortly after and said that the same ex-priest who had once counseled her had asked her out for coffee. What did I think? I remember urging her to go, as here was someone with the spiritual and activist grounding to match my wonderful friend. As you will have discovered from this story, only John an ex-radical theologian could have provided the insight into that question, and understood her long struggle.

When they met again, John was a widow and Robin was ready to open her heart again. John didn't just embrace Robin and Nikki into his life, but their whole community — and vice versa. I was one of the lucky ones to be swept into that constellation. One of John's inspirations, quantum physicist David Bohm, said that an acorn is like a portal through which energy and matter pass to create the oak tree. John and Robin have created a portal through which all our energy and yours can pass to create an oak tree of support for this battered world.

Briony Penn

Best Columnist and Feature Writer in Western Canada, 2001,
Television broadcaster and host of Enviro/Mental, Author of the BC
Bestseller "Year on the Wild Side", published by Horsdal & Schubart

CPSIA information can be obtained at www.ICGtesting.com
Printed in the USA
LVOW091422281111

256800LV00006B/1/P